THE RHINE CYCLE ROUTE

FROM SOURCE TO SEA

About the Author

Mike Wells has been a keen cyclist for over 20 years. Starting with UK Sustrans routes, like Lon Las Cymru in Wales and the C2C route across northern England, he soon moved on to long-distance routes in continental Europe and beyond. These include cycling both the Camino and Ruta de la Plata to Santiago de la Compostela, a traverse of Cuba from end to end, a circumnavigation of Iceland and a trip across Lapland to the North Cape.

While working for a travel company he made frequent visits to various parts of the Rhine Valley and saw the cycle-friendly infrastructure all along the river. This inspired him to cycle the route for the first time with his partner Christine. In researching this book, Mike cycled the length of the river three more times, following cycle routes along both banks and exploring other alternatives.

Other Cicerone guides by the author
The Adlerweg: The Eagle's Way across the Austrian Tyrol

THE RHINE CYCLE ROUTE

FROM SOURCE TO SEA

by Mike Wells

CICERONE

2 POLICE SQUARE, MILNTHORPE, CUMBRIA LA7 7PY
www.cicerone.co.uk

© Mike Wells 2013
First edition 2013
ISBN: 978 1 85284 691 6

Printed by KHL Printing, Singapore.

A catalogue record for this book is available from the British Library.

All photographs are by the author unless otherwise stated.

*In memory of my parents, who first took
me along the Rhine in 1960, aged 11.
At the time I did not appreciate it fully.
I have learnt differently since.*

Advice to Readers

While every effort is made by our authors to ensure the accuracy of guidebooks as they go to print, changes can occur during the lifetime of an edition. If we know of any, there will be an Updates tab on this book's page on the Cicerone website (www.cicerone.co.uk), so please check before planning your trip. We also advise that you check information about such things as transport, accommodation and shops locally. Even rights of way can be altered over time. We are always grateful for information about any discrepancies between a guidebook and the facts on the ground, sent by email to info@cicerone.co.uk or by post to Cicerone, 2 Police Square, Milnthorpe LA7 7PY, United Kingdom.

Front cover: Cycling past Marksburg Castle in the Rhine Gorge (Stage 17)

CONTENTS

MAP KEY

start of route		route	
end of route		alternative route	
start/finish point		route direction	
built-up area		alternative route direction	
forested area		tourist information	
international border (on city maps)		railway station	
927km Rhine km cumulative distance		bus station	
40 knooppunten waypoint		youth hostel	
✳ viewpoint		cathedral	
ferry crossing		castle	
airport		point of interest	

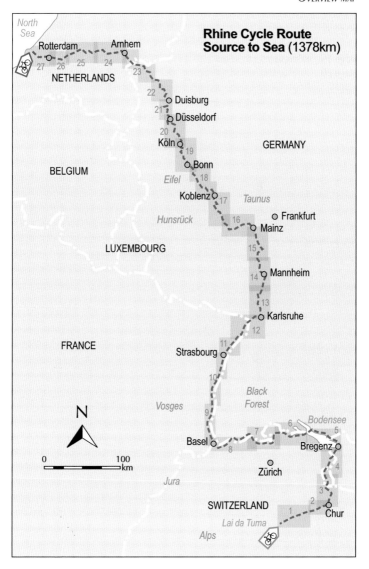

The Rhine near Remagen with the ruined stump of
Ludendorff railway bridge in the background (Stage 18)

INTRODUCTION

Church at Rueras (Stage 1)

The great attraction of following a river from source to sea is that it is downhill all the way (well, almost all the way – our route does occasionally climb a little for spectacular views down into the valley). From the summit of Oberalppass (which can be reached by cycle-friendly train), near the source of the river at Lai da Tuma, the Rhine Cycle Route descends 2046m to the North Sea at Hoek van Holland (Hook of Holland), 1378km distant. The cycling is straightforward, with much of the route following well-surfaced cycle tracks, often along the riverbank or flood dykes. On those occasions where roads are used, these are usually quiet country routes with dedicated cycle lanes. All the countries it passes through are highly cycle-friendly, and motorists will generally give you plenty of room. This route is suitable both for experienced long-distance cyclists and those who have done only a little cycle touring and wish to attempt something more adventurous.

The route mostly follows Swiss, German, French and Dutch national cycle trails, with a high standard of waymarking throughout. This guide breaks the route into 27 stages, averaging just over 50km per stage. A fit cyclist, covering two stages per day, should be able to complete the trip in two weeks. A more leisurely 80km per day would allow some sightseeing and you would still complete the journey in 17 days. You can break the journey at almost any point as there are many places to stay along the way. These are suitable for all budgets, varying from 35 Hostelling International youth hostels (and many backpacker hostels) to B&Bs, guesthouses and hotels. If you do not mind the extra weight of camping gear, there are many official campsites.

The Rhine is rightly one of the world's greatest rivers and one of the most visited by tourists. Many travel by boat, disembarking only at tourist honey-pots and eating international food on-board. By cycling the length of the river you will have a completely different perspective, passing through smaller towns, meeting local people and eating local food. English is widely spoken, almost universally in Switzerland and the Netherlands.

This is a journey of variety. Passing through six countries (Switzerland, Germany, France and the Netherlands, with short sections in Liechtenstein and Austria) you will be exposed to much of the geography, history, culture and economic success of Western Europe.

From the River Rhine's upper reaches in Switzerland, surrounded by high Alpine mountains, our route passes the tiny principality of Liechtenstein to reach Bodensee (Lake Constance), Western Europe's second-largest natural lake. On the shores of Bodensee are the Austrian festival town of Bregenz, where open-air opera is presented every summer on a stage over the water, and Friedrichshafen, home to the Zeppelin. Beyond the lake is Rheinfall, continental Europe's largest waterfall by volume of water. Below here the river flows through an attractive wooded valley between the Black Forest and the Jura mountains, passing a series of unspoilt medieval towns. After Basel, the route turns north through French Alsace, an area much fought over, with many remnants of successive wars. Then it is on past the French gastronomic centre of Strasbourg, the great industrial cities of Karlsruhe and Mannheim/Ludwigshafen, and the imperial cities and religious centres of Speyer, Worms and Mainz, before reaching the barrier of the Taunus and Hunsrück mountains. The Rhine Gorge, cutting between these ranges, is the most spectacular stage of all, lined with fairy-tale castles and award-winning vineyards. Halfway through is the infamous Loreley (or Lorelei) Rock. Continuing between the dormant volcanic Eifel and Siebengebirge ranges, where an active geyser demonstrates the power of vulcanism, the Rhine emerges onto the North German Plain.

The route continues to Bonn, past the Bundeshaus (where the West German parliament sat from 1949 to 1999) and Beethoven's birthplace, then on to Köln (Cologne), with over

St Goarshausen, seen from the Loreley Rock (Stage 17)

1 million inhabitants the largest city en route and site of the world's tallest cathedral spire. Then past Düsseldorf and through the industrial city of Duisburg, which produces half of all German steel and is Europe's largest inland port. For most of the way through this area, the river is followed, avoiding much of the intensive industrial development. Continuing through wide open flat agricultural land into the Netherlands, the river starts dividing to eventually reach the North Sea by way of five different channels. Our route follows one of these, the Lek, cycling on top of flood dykes with intensively farmed polders, lower than the river and reclaimed over many centuries, lining the river's course. At Kinderdijk there are 19 surviving windmills of

the type used to drain this land. The last great city is Rotterdam, rebuilt hurriedly after destruction in the Second World War and now being rebuilt again with much stunning modern architecture. On the opposite bank, between Rotterdam and the North Sea is Europoort, which was the world's busiest port until overtaken by Shanghai in 2004.

BACKGROUND

Throughout this guide the English spelling of Rhine is used, except for in proper nouns such as Rheinquelle, Canal du Rhône au Rhin, Neder Rijn, where the appropriate national spelling is used. On the maps, Rhein is used in German-speaking areas, Rhin in France and Rijn in the Netherlands.

The cycle track past the Kinderdijk windmills is very popular (Stage 26)

Geographically the Rhine has six distinct sections:

- **Alpenrhein** (Alpine Rhine) is the combination of the Vorderrhein and Hinterrhein tributaries that flow rapidly down the north side of the Alps, along deep glacial valleys, into Bodensee.
- **Hochrhein** (Higher Rhine) continues descending through broad wooded gorges providing the border between Switzerland and Baden-Württemberg (Germany) from Bodensee to Basel.
- **Oberrhein** (Upper Rhine) meanders north from Basel across a broad plain, between the Vosges mountains in French Alsace and the German Black Forest, as far as Mainz.
- **Mittelrhein** (Middle Rhine) is a picturesque stretch from Mainz to Bonn, where the river has cut

the Rhine Gorge between the Hunsrück/Eifel mountains (west) and the Taunus/Siebengebirge ranges (east).

- **Niederrhein** (Lower Rhine) crosses the North German Plain from Bonn to the Dutch border.
- **Delta Rijn** (Rhine Delta) is the Dutch part of the river, which divides into five different arms to reach the North Sea.

However, the Rhine is more than just a river. Flowing through the heart of Western Europe, it has significance far beyond its relatively modest 1232km length. It can be described as four rivers in one. Firstly it functions as an important national border; secondly it is the source of many of the myths and legends central to European culture; thirdly it is a great commercial artery and location for industry; and fourthly it has a magnetic attraction to tourists and pursuers of leisure activities.

The border Rhine

For two millennia, the river has represented the border between major national entities. The Romans set their northern frontier along the Rhine/Danube axis and established the first towns on the Rhine at Colonia (Köln), Mainz, Strasbourg and Xanten as bases for legions defending their empire against barbarian tribes to the east. By medieval times this demarcation had developed into a border between Germanic speaking nations of the Holy Roman Empire, east of the river, and Francophone ones to the west. From the Middle Ages up to the mid-20th century, continuing power struggles saw frequent territorial claims and border incursions.

Further south, Swiss, Austrians and Bavarians competed to control the northern approaches to the Alps, with the Rhine becoming a natural boundary between their interests. In the far north, both the Dutch and Spanish used the river in their struggle for hegemony over the Netherlands.

As a result, the river is peppered with military hardware from Roman fortifications, through medieval castles, fortified military towns and integrated defensive lines to concrete anti-tank defences, each passing into history as the technological progress of warfare made them redundant. Riverside settlements still show the scars of battle, particularly from the Second World War, where intensive bombing was followed by destructive land warfare. This is particularly evident in relation to the bridges. In the

The German town of Laufenburg, on the north bank of the Rhine (Stage 8)

mid-19th century, the Prussian military authorities controlling the Rhineland resisted the construction of railway bridges as a potential danger of invasion. Before and during the First World War German forces constructed a series of mighty bridges to support the war in France, only to destroy them in 1944/45 in an attempt to prevent Allied invasion of Germany.

The legendary Rhine

The oldest tales of the Rhine are derived from the *Nibelungenlied*, a 13th-century poem by an unknown German author. It centred on the bloodthirsty affairs of court in Worms and featured Siegfried, Brunhilde and a hoard of gold that caused much strife and was eventually buried in the Rhine to prevent further trouble.

Siegfried went on to feature in many other legends. Composer Richard Wagner (1813–1883) used this tale for the basis of Das Rheingold and subsequent works making up The Ring of the Nibelung opera cycle.

Many of the towns, villages and castles along the German part of the river have local legends, some of which are related in the route description. Perhaps the most famous is the song of the Loreley maiden. First appearing in 1801, the story was rewritten by the author Heinrich Heine in 1824 and set to music in 1837.

The Rhine provided the inspiration for two great patriotic songs. *La Marseillaise*, the French national anthem, was written in Strasbourg in 1792 as a 'War song for the Army of

Blockhouse turret on the Maginot Line at Marckolsheim (Stage 10)

Cruise boat passing Loreley maiden (Stage 17)

the Rhine' to honour troops defending post-revolutionary France from Prussian and Austrian invasion. On the German side, the poem/song *Die Wacht am Rhein* ('The Guard on the Rhine') was written in 1840 as a call to arms following French political moves to extend French territory. During the Franco-Prussian war (1870–71) it became an unofficial German anthem and remained popular until the Second World War, although it is rarely heard nowadays.

The commercial Rhine

Although used from Roman times as a freight transport route, medieval use of the river was limited by rapids, shallows and local tolls collected at over 200 toll stations. These toll stations were swept away by the Congress of Vienna in 1815, while a series of river improvements throughout the 19th and 20th centuries have removed barriers to navigation on the Mittelrhein and canalised much of the Oberrhein. Steam navigation commenced in 1840 as far as Mannheim, but it was nearly 100 years before improvements allowed commercial operations to reach Basel. Today, thousands of boats and barges carry approximately 250 million tonnes of merchandise annually, including coal, oil, ore, chemicals, building materials and manufactured goods. Major flows are from the huge ports of Rotterdam and Europoort to Duisburg, Köln, Mannheim, Karlsruhe, Strasbourg and Basel. Canals linking the Rhine with the neighbouring river catchments of the Elbe, Danube, Marne and Rhône enable trans-European waterway transport.

*Two railways, two roads and a cycle track follow
the river through the Rhine Gorge (Stage 17)*

Ease of transportation has encouraged industrial development all along the navigable river. Most noticeable is the chemical industry, with 20% of the world's chemicals produced at a number of huge integrated chemical works, including BASF at Ludwigshafen, the world's largest single company chemical plant.

The leisure Rhine
Millions of tourists visit the Rhine every year. Many come by road to see great tourist sights such as Köln, the Rhine Gorge, Rüdesheim, Speyer, Strasbourg and the Rheinfall. Others come to cycle round, sail on, swim in or just laze beside Bodensee, southern Germany's principal resort area.

Rhine cruising in large all-inclusive boats is big business and many companies operate in this area. Cruises typically follow seven-day itineraries between Amsterdam and Basel (or back), stopping at principal cities along the way. At popular locations up to 10 boats may call every day. Short-trip and day excursion boats operate on a few stretches, particularly between Köln and Mainz, Schaffhausen and Konstanz and on Bodensee.

Leisure activities are numerous. Almost every town has a public swimming pool, often beside the river. White-water rafting is possible through Ruinaulta (Stage 2), while Huningue (Stage 9) has a canoe slalom course. Rowing and sailing clubs abound.

Cycling is one of the most popular leisure activities in all of the countries of the Rhine, particularly in places like Bodensee, the Rhine Gorge and Kinderdijk, where cyclists of all ages and degrees of fitness can be seen. Cycling as a family holiday is popular in Germany.

Physical geography
Two major geomorphic events shaped the Rhine basin. The Alps were formed approximately 30 million years ago, pushed up by the collision of the African and European tectonic plates. This caused rippling of the landmass to the north, creating successive ridges that form the limestone Jura (northern Switzerland) and combined Vosges (France)/Black Forest (Germany). Further north, pre-existing harder slate mountains (Hunsrück/Taunus) and volcanic remnants (Eifel, Siebengebirge and Westerwald) were raised further. The Rhine, flowing north from the Alps, was forced west by the barrier of the Black Forest, then turned north, cutting a wide valley between Vosges and the Black Forest (from modern-day Basel to Karlsruhe). Flowing slowly across the basin between the ridges (Karlsruhe to Mainz), the river deposited much of its sediment, creating an extensive flood plain. Upon reaching the Taunus, it turned west then north again, cutting a narrow gorge through the older, harder rocks between Taunus and Hunsrück (forming the Rhine Gorge

from Bingen to Koblenz). Emerging from the mountains, the Rhine flows out onto the North German Plain.

The second event was a period of glaciation known as the ice ages, ending around 14,000 years ago. This had three effects upon the Rhine basin. In the Alps great glaciers formed, cutting deep, straight valleys from Oberalp to Chur and Chur to Bodensee, a lake which formed at the end of the glacier. Further north, ice sheets covered the North German Plain, which when they retreated left a flat landscape covered with glacial and wind-blown deposits. Furthermore, when the ice sheets melted, the sea rose, leaving the western end of the plain (modern-day Netherlands) below sea level.

Stork nest at Willige Langerak (Stage 25)

Wildlife

While a number of small mammals (including rabbits, hares, red squirrels, voles, water rats and weasels) may be seen scuttling across the track and deer may be glimpsed in forests, this is not a route for observing animals. However, there is a wide range of interesting birdlife. White swans, geese and many varieties of ducks inhabit the river and its banks. Cruising above, raptors, particularly buzzards and kites, are frequently seen hunting small mammals, with kites diving occasionally into the river to catch fish. Other birds that live by fishing include cormorants, noticeable when perched on rocks with their wings spread out to dry, and kingfishers. These are found in

many locations, mostly on backwaters, perching where they can observe the water. Despite their bright blue and orange plumage they are very difficult to spot. Grey herons, on the other hand, are very visible. Common all along the Rhine, and particularly numerous in the Netherlands, they can be seen standing in shallow water waiting to strike or stalking purposefully along the banks.

Perhaps the most noticeable birds are white storks. These huge birds, with wingspan of 2 metres, nest in trees or on man-made platforms. They feed on small mammals and reptiles, which they catch in water meadows or on short grassland. Populations along the Rhine dropped to unsustainable levels by the 1980s, but conservation programmes in France, Germany and the Netherlands have led to significant growth in numbers and white storks are no longer regarded as a threatened species.

THE ROUTE

For much of its 1232km length it is possible to cycle along either bank of the Rhine. In preparing this book, the author followed both banks and explored some alternative routes away from the river. While the route described here mostly follows the left (southern or western) bank, various deviations are made, which are personal selections of the author. The total distance cycled by the route described in this book is 1378km.

Where possible, rural or parkland routes are preferred to urban ones. Although a number of large cities are traversed, few require significant lengths of urban street cycling. In three cities, dedicated cycle tracks along canal banks (Strasbourg), linear city parks (Karlsruhe) or through urban woodland (Mannheim) take the route into the heart of the city without encountering traffic. In eight others (Bregenz, Konstanz, Schaffhausen, Mainz, Koblenz, Bonn, Köln, and Düsseldorf), the route sticks to the river as it passes close by the city centres.

Between cities, traffic-free routes are preferred over road ones, surfaced tracks over dirt ones, scenic tracks over dull ones and tracks that stay true to the river over those cutting off significant chunks for the sake of it. Deviations are made to visit places of significant interest, such as Heidiland (Stage 3), the north side of Bodensee (Stage 5), Waldshut and Bad Säckingen (Stage 7), Neuf-Brisach

Werdenberg, the smallest town in Switzerland (Stage 4)

(Stage 9), Karlsruhe (Stage 12), the Rheingau (Stage 16), Oosterbeek (Stage 24) and Kinderdijk (Stage 26).

Switzerland

From Oberalppass to Bodensee Rhein Delta, the Swiss national cycle route Radweg 2 (R2) is closely followed through Ilanz and Chur. R2 passes Vaduz in Liechtenstein on the opposite side of the river, but the route in this guide crosses over to visit Europe's third-smallest country. R2 is left for a long deviation along Bodensee Radweg around the northern side of Bodensee, visiting Friedrichshafen, home of the Zeppelin, and the medieval cities of Lindau and Meersburg. Between Bodensee and Basel, where the Rhine mostly provides the border between Switzerland and Germany, R2 is followed through quaint Stein am Rhein, the German enclave of Büsingen, Schaffhausen, and the spectacular Rheinfall. We briefly leave R2, crossing into Germany to visit Waldshut and Bad Säckingen. Regaining the Swiss bank through Rheinfelden and Roman Augusta Raurica, R2 ends in Basel.

France

From Basel to Strasbourg (France) and its sister town of Kehl (Germany) there are three alternative routes. This guide follows the waymarked French Rhin route (RR), leaving the river to follow canal towpaths, forest trails and a disused railway line through Alsace, passing Neuf-Brisach en route to Strasbourg. There is another waymarked route (D8) closely following the German (right) bank through Breisach to Kehl. This is shorter, but is a dusty, bumpy dirt track for most of its length and is not recommended. The third alternative is to follow quiet country roads along the French bank of the Rhine.

Germany

After Strasbourg the route continues following RR, now along the riverbank, through the French/German border area before crossing the river to visit the model fan-shaped city of Karlsruhe. It is possible to continue along the left bank through Wörth, but major works are going on in this area to create flood relief polders and deviations take the track away from the river. Returning to the left bank after Karlsruhe, the route passes through Germersheim and the cathedral city of Speyer, then crosses over briefly to visit Mannheim (and miss the duller part of Ludwigshafen). Then it is back on the left bank through Worms and Nierstein to reach Mainz, the most attractive 'big city' on the Rhine. For most of the stretch between Karlsruhe and Mainz through Mannheim it is possible to follow D8 along the right bank, but while this is a quiet route along surfaced tracks, it is far less interesting than the preferred left bank RR route.

The river is crossed at Mainz for the short stretch to Rüdesheim. From Bingen, the route stays on the left bank through the Rhine Gorge, passing romantic castles and the Loreley Rock opposite. The route continues north, crossing the Mosel at Koblenz then past the Eifel mountains through Andernach and Remagen. A brief crossing to visit Königswinter below the Drachenfels, then back on the left bank past Bonn, which marks a major change in the landscape. The mountains are left behind for the plains of Nordrhein-Westfalen. From Bonn, through Köln and Düsseldorf to Duisburg you pass through the industrial heart of Germany. However, apart from the approach to Duisburg past a series of steelworks, the stretches between cities are surprisingly rural. Beyond Köln, we cross the river to visit Düsseldorf (attractive) and Duisburg (industrial). The final stretch in Germany crosses wide open agricultural plains following a series of flood dykes on the left bank with occasional glimpses of the river as it meanders widely towards the Dutch border at Millingen.

The Netherlands

After reaching the Netherlands, the Rhine divides into different channels to reach the sea. The main route followed by this guide crosses the Waal, then follows the Neder Rijn past Arnhem and the Lek to Rotterdam. From Arnhem to Amerongen the route follows the right bank between a ridge of sandy wooded hills and the river, while beyond Amerongen the route is along the top of the main flood dyke alongside the Lek, with the surrounding land below sea level. Beyond Amerongen, an alternative route bears right, continuing through Utrecht to follow the Oude Rijn to Leiden and the sea at Katwijk. This pleasant winding river was the original route of the Rhine until its course was altered by medieval floods. At Wijk bij Duurstede, another alternative – the Rijn Delta route – crosses the Lek then follows the Linge, another attractive old river, before crossing the Waal and Biesbosch polder to Dordrecht and Rotterdam. Beyond Rotterdam, the route ends at the North Sea ferry port of Hoek van Holland, near the river mouth.

PREPARATION

When to go

Apart from the higher parts of Stage 1, where snow often lingers on the ground until May and fresh snow can fall at any time, the route is generally cycleable from April to October. Indeed, much of the route can be cycled at any time of year. The river is at its highest in winter, after heavy snowfalls, when snow melt coming down from the Alps can cause localised flooding of the route in a few places where it drops down below the flood dyke.

During July and August (the school holiday season) some of the more touristic stages can become very busy, particularly Stages 5 and 6 around Bodensee and Stages 16 and 17 through the Rhine Gorge. Although these stages have a large number of places to stay, it is sometimes difficult

Oberalppass closed by snow in April (Stage 1)

to find accommodation, especially at weekends.

How long will it take?
The route has been broken into 27 stages averaging 51km per stage. Cycling 100km per day would enable you to complete the route in two weeks. Allowing time for sightseeing and averaging 80km per day would stretch this time to 17 days. At a leisurely pace of one stage (50km) per day, it would take four weeks to complete the ride. On most stages there are many places to stay and it is easy to tailor daily distances to your requirements.

What kind of cycle is suitable?
While most of the route is on surfaced cycle tracks or roads (usually asphalt, but some concrete and in northern Germany and the Netherlands long stretches of brick-block), there are some stretches of all-weather dirt, cinder or gravel track. As a result, this is not a route for narrow-tyred racing cycles. The ideal cycle is a hybrid (a lightweight but strong cross between a touring cycle and a mountain bike with at least 21 gears), although apart from Disentis/Mustér to Ilanz (Stage 1) and Worms to Oppenheim (Stage 15) a touring cycle would be quite suitable. For both these stages an alternative route exists along local roads. Front suspension is beneficial as it absorbs much of the vibration. Straight handlebars, with bar-ends enabling you to vary your position regularly, are recommended. Make sure your cycle is serviced and lubricated before you start, particularly the brakes, gears and chain.

As important as the cycle is your choice of tyres. Slick road tyres are not suitable and knobbly mountain bike tyres not necessary. What you need is something in-between with good tread and a slightly wider profile than you would use for everyday cycling at home. To reduce the chance of punctures, choose tyres with puncture resistant armouring, such as a Keflar band.

GETTING THERE AND BACK

By air
The easiest way to reach Oberalppass is to fly to Zürich. A number of airlines offer direct flights from various airports in the UK and continental Europe. Airlines have different requirements regarding how cycles are presented and some, but not all, make a charge – which you should pay when booking as it is usually higher if you pay at the airport. All airlines require tyres to be partially deflated, handlebars turned and pedals removed (loosen pedals beforehand to make them easier to remove at the airport). Most will accept your cycle in a transparent polythene bike-bag, but some insist on you using a cardboard bike-box. These can be obtained from cycle shops, usually for free. You do, however, have the problem of how you get the box to the airport!

From Zürich airport, frequent SBB trains run to Zürich Hauptbahnhof (central station), with hourly connections to Göschenen. In general, cycle provision in Swiss trains is excellent and reservations are not normally required. However, some services from Zürich Hauptbahnhof use SBB ICN or CIS units (high-speed trains) with limited cycle provision. These are indicated in both Swiss and international timetables. From Göschenen, MGB narrow-gauge trains run steeply uphill through the Reuss Gorge to Andermatt, where connecting hourly MGB trains take you on to Oberalppass. Glacier Express trains also run between Andermatt and Oberalppass, but have no cycle space. Discounted through tickets can be bought in advance through www. sbb.ch. Cycle tickets cost CHF15 and cover all journeys within a day.

By rail
On the surface rail looks the easiest, but not necessarily the cheapest, option. However, there is a problem. Many of the most convenient long-distance services across Europe are operated by high-speed trains that have either very limited provision for cycles (Eurostar) or no space at all (French TGV and Thalys, German ICE, Swiss ICN and CIS). Eurostar will carry your cycle from London to Paris or Brussels, but it must be boxed and they do not guarantee conveying it by the same train as you! In Germany, IC (Inter City) and EC (Euro City) trains have reservable cycle space and can be used to reach Basel or Zürich. Cycle tickets should be purchased in

advance, even if passenger reservations are not required.

From the UK, conventional trains can be used to reach either Folkestone (for Eurotunnel) or Dover (for cross channel ferries). On Eurotunnel shuttles, cycles are carried inside a special vehicle (maximum six cycles) on two departures daily. This vehicle picks up from the Folkestone/Channel Tunnel Holiday Inn Express hotel in Cheriton at 0800 and 1530. The hotel is a short ride from Folkestone West station. For more information see www.eurotunnel.com, but bookings must be made by phone (tel: 01303 282201). Dover ferry terminal is a short ride from Dover Priory railway station. P&O provides frequent sailings to Calais, all of which convey cycles. Bookings can be made through www.poferries.com.

From Calais Ville station, SNCF Corail trains with cycle spaces run to Paris Gare du Nord. A very short ride takes you to Paris Gare de l'Est for trains to Strasbourg and Basel. Most services on this route are operated by TGV or ICE high-speed trains, but there are some conventional Corail services that convey cycles. Regular Swiss SBB trains with cycle space run between Basel and Göschenen, but some require you to change at Arth Goldau. For connections between Göschenen and Oberalppass see 'By air'. Booking for French trains is through Rail Europe www.raileurope.co.uk. Swiss trains do not require reservation, but discounted tickets are

Loading a cycle onto a Swiss train

available in advance through www. sbb.ch. In Switzerland, a one-day ticket is required for your cycle.

An alternative if starting from the UK is to use ferries to reach Hoek van Holland from Harwich or Rotterdam from Hull, then Dutch NS trains to Utrecht, were you join the overnight Amsterdam to Zürich train, with reservable cycle spaces. On Hoek van Holland ferries, through tickets allow you to travel from London (or any station in East Anglia) to any station in the Netherlands.

By road

If you are lucky to have someone willing to drop you off at the start, it is between 900km and 950km from Calais to Oberalppass (depending upon the route taken), which is on Swiss Route 19 between Andermatt and Chur.

European Bike Express operates a coach service with a dedicated cycle trailer from northern England, picking up en route across England to the Mediterranean. Handlebars need turning, but otherwise cycles remain intact. There are convenient drop-off points in eastern France at Nancy or Mâcon; details and booking can be found at www.bike-express.co.uk. In Nancy you can join the Paris to Strasbourg train service, then continue as described in 'By rail'. From Mâcon by SNCF train to Geneva, then SBB train to Brig and MGB narrow-gauge train to Oberalppass. All these services convey cycles, except for Glacier Express trains between Brig and Oberalppass.

Intermediate access

There are international airports at Friedrichshafen (Stage 5), Basel/Mulhouse/Freiburg (Stage 9), Strasbourg (Stage 10), Karlsruhe/Baden (Stage 12), Köln/Bonn (Stage 19) and Düsseldorf (Stage 21). Zürich airport is 14km from Teufen (Stage 7) and Frankfurt airport 24km from Mainz (Stage 16) (note: Frankfurt Hahn airport is in the Hunsrück mountains 50km west of Bacharach and is not close to the route). Düsseldorf Weeze is 18km from Kalkar (Stage 23). Amsterdam Schiphol airport can be reached by train from Arnhem and Rhenen.

Much of the route through Switzerland and Germany is closely followed by railway lines. In France between Basel and Strasbourg the railway is some distance from the route and in the Netherlands there are no lines following the river and stations are only encountered at Arnhem, Rhenen and between Rotterdam and Hoek van Holland. Stations en route are listed in the text.

Onward travel from Hoek van Holland

Trains from Hoek van Holland run to Rotterdam, where frequent connections serve Amsterdam Schiphol, a major international airport with flights to worldwide destinations.

Stena Line runs two ferries daily from Hoek van Holland to Harwich in the UK, in the afternoon and overnight (www.stenaline.co.uk). On overnight sailings, passengers must reserve cabins. From Harwich, trains with cycle provision run to London (Liverpool St) and to Cambridge, where connections are available to the rest of the UK.

P&O ferries sail every night from Rotterdam (Europoort) to Hull (www.poferries.com). To reach the P&O terminal, cross the Rhine by the Maassluis–Rozenburg ferry and follow LF1 signs through Rozenburg. Turn right following a cycle track on the left of Europaweg for 9km to reach the terminal at berth 5805 (Rozenburg ferry ramp to port 11.5km).

NAVIGATION

Waymarking

The route described in this guide is made up from various national waymarked cycle routes plus some locally signposted stretches to link these together. In a few places, the route varies from that waymarked where the author believes an alternative route is preferable. The style and consistency of waymarking varies from country to country and stage to stage. In the introduction to each stage an indication is given of the predominant waymarks followed.

In Switzerland, waymarking is excellent and ubiquitous with a well-developed national system integrating cycle routes, mountain bike trails and footpaths. The letter R (for Radweg or cycle way) and colour maroon indicate cycle routes. Full details and maps of all Swiss waymarked routes can be found at www.veloland. ch. Judith and Neil Forsyth's *Cycle Touring in Switzerland* (Cicerone Press) describes the nine national routes R1 to R9. When in Switzerland, this guide closely follows R2 'Rhein route' from Oberalppass to Basel (Stages 1–4 and 6–8), except for some deviations to visit places of interest across the river.

In Germany, local waymarking is excellent but national waymarking variable. This is influenced by Germany's federal structure of semi-independent *lände*, or states, each of which has its own system. A national cycle network is in existence, although this often plays second fiddle to regional and local routes, with some signposts carrying the badges of many different routes. National route

SUMMARY OF NATIONAL CYCLE ROUTES FOLLOWED

R2	Radweg 2 (Rhein route)	Switzerland
BR	Bodensee Radweg	Switzerland/Austria/Germany
D8	Deutsche Radweg 8	Germany
RR	Veloroute Rhin/Rhein	France/Germany
LF+number	Landelijkefiets	The Netherlands

(clockwise) German D8 sign; EU veloroute Rhin sign (used in France); Dutch Landeslijkefiets sign; Swiss R2 Rhein route sign

27

Dutch Knooppunt (waypoint) sign

D8 follows the Rhine, mostly on the eastern (right) bank, and on some stages this is followed. The Bodensee Radweg (BR) encircles Bodensee and is followed on Stages 5 and 6. From Karlsruhe to Mainz (Stages 12–15), European Rhin/Rhein Route signs are encountered (see France below) and these are found occasionally as far north as the Dutch border. In most lände, cycle route signposts have a white background, but the text colour varies (green in Bavaria, Baden-Württemberg, Rheinland-Pfalz and Hessen; red in Nordrhein-Westfalen).

France has adopted a proposed European waymarking system using blue/white signs with the European yellow stars/blue ground symbol to identify 'Rhin Route' (RR), with comprehensive waymarking funded by an EU grant. This route is followed, with a few small deviations, from Basel to Lauterbourg (Stages 9–12), continuing through Germany to Mainz (spelt Mayence on French signposts).

Unsurprisingly, the Netherlands, a country with more cycles than people, has an excellent waymarked national cycle network known as Landelijkefiets-routes (LF). Full details can be found at www.nederland fietsland.nl. This guide uses parts of LF3 (Millingen to Arnhem, Stage 23), LF4 (Arnhem to Amerongen, Stage 24), LF11 (Ablasserdam to Rotterdam, Stage 26) and LF12 (Rotterdam to Hoek van Holland, Stage 27). Signposts include a or b after the route number to indicate direction. Where this guide does not use LF routes (Amerongen to Ablasserdam, Stages 24–26), local signposting is excellent. In addition there is a system of *knooppunten* (nodal waypoints) with numbered location boards and local maps spread throughout the country. These actually start in Germany 10km before the Dutch border.

Maps
The most comprehensive coverage of the whole route is provided by Esterbauer Bikeline cycling guides (see below), which include strip maps of the entire route at 1:75,000. These do not cover the route around Bodensee (Stage 5), that through Karlsruhe (Stages 12 and 13) or the

long section across the Netherlands from Amerongen to Ablasserdam (Stages 24–26).

The only stand-alone maps of the whole route from source to Rotterdam plus Bodensee Radweg are published by Publicpress (www.publicpress.de), who produce a series of five plastic laminated folding strip maps: Publicpress maps 199, 302, 368, 333 and 569. Although these are 1:50,000, they contain less detail and are less accurate than Bikeline guides.

For Switzerland, including the part of the route across the river in Germany and the northern side of Bodensee, detailed maps of R2, at any scale you wish, can be downloaded from www.veloland.ch.

For France, Bikeline publish two sheets at 1:75,000 (Radkarte Elsass Süd and Elsass Nord) covering the route from Basel to north of Karlsruhe.

For Germany, Bikeline publish a map at 1:75,000 covering Bodensee, one covering Konstanz to Basel, three maps covering the stretch from Karlsruhe to Koblenz and one covering Düsseldorf to Millingen: Bikeline RK sheets BW08, BW13, BW03, RPF06, HES4 and NRW3. Publicpress publish six sheets at 1:100,000 covering the route from Karlsruhe to Millingen: Publicpress sheets 168, 120, 576, 157, 228 and 166. Bikeline maps contain more detail and are more accurate.

For the Netherlands both ANWB (Dutch automobile association) and Falk/VVV (Dutch tourist office) publish a series of 1:50,000 *fietskaarten* (cycle maps) covering the route from Millingen to Hoek van Holland: ANWB sheets 10, 15 and 14, with a very short section on sheet 11; Falk/VVV sheets 11 and 15. Both sets of maps provide good coverage. The ANWB maps are the most recommended.

Other guidebooks

Bikeline publish three Radtourenbücher und Karte (cycle tour guidebooks with maps) covering the whole route as far as Rotterdam, excluding the northern side of Bodensee (www.esterbauer.com). These provide much information but are only available in German: Vol. 1 Andermatt to Basel, Vol. 2 Basel to Mainz and Vol. 3 Mainz to Rotterdam. A separate book covers the Bodensee Radweg.

Although neither a map nor guidebook, a topographic strip map of the Rhine from Bodensee to Rotterdam produced by Rahmelverlag (www.rahmel-verlag.de) gives a good overall impression of the route and makes an attractive souvenir. It is published in a number of languages, including English, and is sold in gift shops along the route, particularly in Rüdesheim and Boppard.

Most of these maps and guidebooks are available from leading bookshops including Stanfords in London (www.stanfords.co.uk) and The Map Shop, Upton upon Severn (www.themapshop.co.uk). Relevant maps are widely available en route.

Hotels, inns, guest houses, and bed & breakfast

For most of the route there is a wide variety of accommodation. Hotels vary from expensive five-star properties to modest local establishments. Hotels and inns usually offer a full meal service, guest houses do sometimes. B&Bs, which in Germany and Switzerland can be recognised by a sign *zimmer frei* (rooms available), generally offer only breakfast. Tourist information offices will normally telephone for you and make local reservations. After hours, many tourist offices display a sign outside showing local establishments with vacancies. Booking ahead is seldom necessary, except on popular stages in high season, but it is advisable to start looking for accommodation soon after 1600. Most properties are cycle-friendly and will find you a secure overnight place for your pride and joy.

Prices vary between countries, with Switzerland the most expensive. On stages following the Swiss–German border, it is cheaper to cross to the German side of the river for overnight accommodation. Compared with equivalent accommodation in the UK, Swiss and Dutch rooms are more expensive, Austrian around the same, and French and German rooms slightly cheaper. One unusual way of overnighting in Switzerland is *schlafen im stroh* (sleeping in the hay), where you stay in a haybarn, often on

Bett+Bike sign

a remote farm. To use this facility you need a sleeping bag and torch. It is strictly no smoking of course!

Bett+Bike

This is a German scheme run by ADFC (German cycling club), which has registered over 5000 establishments providing cycle-friendly accommodation. It includes a wide variety of properties, from major hotels to local B&Bs, listed by state in an annually updated guidebook. Participating establishments display a Bett+Bike sign. For more information visit www.bettundbike.de.

Youth hostels and backpackers

There are 34 official youth hostels (YH), many in historic buildings, on or near the route (4 Swiss, 1 Liechtenstein, 1 Austrian, 2 French, 23 German and 3 Dutch). These are listed in Appendix E. To use a youth hostel you need to be a member of an association affiliated to Hostelling

International. If you are not a member you will be required to join the local association. Rules vary from country to country but generally hostels accept guests of any age, although visitors over 27 may face a small surcharge (€3 in Germany). Rooms vary from single-sex dormitories to family rooms of 2–6 beds. Unlike British hostels, most continental European hostels do not have self-catering facilities but do provide good-value hot meals. Hostels get very busy, particularly during school holidays, and booking is advised through www.hihostels.com.

In Switzerland there are independent backpacker hostels in Disentis/Mustér and Chur. In Germany, France and the Netherlands many cities have backpacker hostels.

Camping

If you are prepared to carry camping equipment, this may appear the cheapest way of cycling the Rhine. However, good-quality campsites with all facilities are often only a little cheaper than B&Bs or hostels. The stage descriptions identify many official campsites but the list is by no means exhaustive. Camping may be possible in other locations with the permission of local landowners.

FOOD AND DRINK

Where to eat

There are thousands of places where cyclists can eat and drink, ranging from snack bars, hotdog stands and local inns to Michelin-starred restaurants. Locations of many places to eat are listed in stage descriptions, but these are by no means exhaustive. Days and times of opening vary. When planning your day, try to be flexible as a number of inns and small restaurants, particularly in German villages, do not open at lunchtime and may have one day a week when they remain closed. A local inn offering food and drink is typically known as a *gaststätte* in German-speaking countries and an *auberge* in France. A *wienstube* is a winebar, often attached to a vineyard. English-language menus are widely available in Switzerland and the Netherlands, but are less common in Germany and France except in larger towns and cities.

When to eat

Breakfast usually consists of breads, jam and a hot drink with, in Germanic areas, the addition of cold meats and cheese and often a boiled egg. In Switzerland the breakfast dish *birchermuesli*, made from rolled oats, nuts and dried fruit, is the forerunner of commercially produced muesli. In Germany lunch was traditionally the main meal of the day, but this is slowly changing, and is unlikely to prove suitable if you plan an afternoon in the saddle. The most common lunchtime snacks everywhere are soups, and ham or cheese sandwiches. In Germany *würst mit senf und brot* (sausages with mustard and bread) and *würstsalat* (thin strips of slicing sausage served with sauerkraut (pickled cabbage)) are popular; while *croque monsieur* (toasted ham/cheese sandwich) and quiche Lorraine are widely available in France.

For dinner, a wide variety of cuisine is available, including Italian, Greek, Turkish and Chinese. Much of what is available is pan-European and will be easily recognisable. There are, however, some national and regional dishes you may wish try.

What to eat

Swiss *rösti* is finely grated potato, fried and often served with bacon and cheese, while *geschnetzeltes* are thin slices of veal in a cream and mushroom sauce usually served with noodles or *rösti*. *Zander* (fresh water pikeperch) is the most commonly found fish in Switzerland. Cheese is popular and is used in *fondue* (melted cheese used as dipping sauce) and *raclette* (grilled slices of cheese drizzled over potatoes and gherkins). As Swiss cooking uses a lot of salt, it is usually worth having a taste before adding any more. Switzerland is rightly famous for chocolate.

Germany is the land of the *schwein* (pig) and dishes of pork, gammon, bacon and ham dominate German menus. Traditionally pork was pot-roasted or grilled rather than fried. There are over 1500 types of German *würst* (sausage), the most common being *bratwürst* (made from minced pork and served grilled or

fried), *Wienerwürst* (smoked sausages served boiled, known as frankfurters in English) and *blutwürst* (blood sausage). *Sauerbraten* is marinated roast beef, while *fleischkaese* and *leberkaese* are kinds of meat loaf. *Forelle* (trout) and *lachs* (salmon) are the most popular fish. The most common vegetable accompaniments are *sauerkraut* and boiled potatoes. *Reibekuchen* are potato pancakes, served with apple sauce. *Spargel* (white asparagus) is consumed in huge quantities during Spargelzeit between mid-April and 24 June. Germans tend to eat cakes mid-morning or mid-afternoon. The most famous German cake is *Schwarzwalder kirschtorte* (Black Forest gateau), a chocolate and cherry cake.

In France, the route is entirely in Alsace, which has a cuisine markedly different to France as a whole, showing strong Germanic influence. Pork is the dominant meat and the most famous Alsatian dish is *choucroute garnie*, a dish of various cuts of pork meat and sausages served with sauerkraut heated in white wine. A typical snack is *tarte flambée* or *flammekueche*, a thin pizza-style base covered with white cheese, onions and bacon and cooked in a wood oven.

Although the variety of dishes offered in Dutch restaurants is generally wider than in Germany, cooking is usually pan-European and traditional Dutch cooking is fairly hard to find. The Dutch eat a lot of fish, including *maatjes* (raw marinated

Tarte flambée, a speciality of Alsace, served with Gewürztraminer white wine

herring), *kibbeling* (deep-fried cod nuggets) and *mosselen* (mussels), the latter two often served with *patats* (chips/French fries) and mayonnaise. The Netherlands is a country of dairy farming and produces a large amount of cheese, the best known varieties being Edam (red, round like a ball) and Gouda (yellow, round like a wheel). Dutch apple cake is a popular dessert.

Drinks

Switzerland, Austria and Germany are predominantly beer-drinking nations, but also produce considerable quantities of wine, while France is a wine-drinking nation where consumption of beer is increasing. The Netherlands produces beer, but no wine.

Switzerland's largest brewery is Feldschlossen, which is passed at Rheinfelden (Stage 8) and can be visited. In Germany, purity laws controlling the production and content of beer have limited the mass consolidation of brewing compared to other European countries, and beer is still brewed in a large number of local breweries. *Pilsener*, a pale lager, is the most widely drunk form, although *weizenbier* (wheat beer), found in both *helles* (pale) and *dunkles* (dark) varieties, is growing in popularity. Very refreshing and slightly sweet tasting, wheat beer is unfiltered and thus naturally cloudy. Distinct local beers are produced in Köln (*kölsch*) and Düsseldorf (*alt*). Glass sizes vary, but common sizes are *kleines* (small,

Traditional way of serving kölsch in a Köln brauhaus (Stage 19)

300ml) and *grosses* (large, half litre). Weizenbier is traditionally served in half litre vase-shaped glasses. *Radler* in Germany is shandy, a 50/50 mix of beer and carbonated lemonade. With a long history of German influence, Alsace is the main beer-producing region of France, with Kronenbourg the largest brewery. The Netherlands has a number or breweries, but is dominated by the Heineken and Amstel lager brands.

Swiss wine is one of the wine-drinking world's great secrets. Substantial quantities of good-quality wine are produced but 98% of this is consumed within the country. Most production is in the Vaud and Valais cantons in the west of the country, although on our route there are vineyards in the Maienfeld hills (Stage 3) and between Schaffhausen and Waldshut (Stage 7). Principal grape varieties are chasselas (white) used for Fendant wine, and pinot noir or blauburgunder (red) used for Dôle wine. German wine production is usually characterised by white wine from the Rhine Valley between Worms and Koblenz, including the side valleys of Nahe and Mosel. The finest German wine comes from the Rheingau, a south-facing ridge between Eltville and Rüdesheim (Stage 16). Reisling grapes are used for the best wines with müller-thurgua for the less distinguished ones. *Trochen* (dry) and *halb-trochen* (medium) varieties are available. Other wine-growing regions passed include the north side of Bodensee around Meersburg (Stage 5), which produces white and rosé wines, and the Ahr Valley (Stage 18), producing the some of the world's most northerly red wines. In France, the east-facing Vosges slopes looking across the Rhine Valley from above Colmar produce strong full-bodied Alsatian white wine from Gewürztraminer grapes.

All the usual soft drinks (colas, lemonade, fruit juices) are widely available. Local specialities include Rivella, a Swiss drink sweetened with lactose (milk sugars), available in a number of varieties. Apple juice mixed 50/50 with carbonated water and known as *apfelschorle* is widely consumed. *Apfelwein* and *most* are cider-like alcoholic drinks produced from apples, particularly around Bodensee.

AMENITIES AND SERVICES

Grocery shops
All cities, towns and larger villages passed through have grocery stores, often supermarkets, and most have pharmacies. Opening hours vary, but grocers in Germany close at 1300 on Saturdays and stay closed all day Sunday. In France they may be closed from 1300 to 1600 daily.

Cycle shops
The route is well provided with cycle shops, most with repair facilities. Locations are listed in the stage descriptions, although this is not exhaustive. In Switzerland, a list of cycle shops can be found at www.veloland.ch. Many cycle shops will adjust brakes and gears, or lubricate your chain, while you wait, often not seeking reimbursement for minor repairs. Touring cyclists should not abuse this generosity and always offer to pay, even if payment is refused.

Currency and banks
Austria, Germany, France and the Netherlands switched from national currencies to Euros (€) in 2002. Switzerland and Liechtenstein use Swiss Francs (CHF). Almost every town has a bank and most have ATM machines that enable you to make transactions in English. Travellers from the UK should contact their banks to confirm activation of bank cards for use in continental Europe. In Switzerland, the best exchange rates are often found at exchange windows in station ticket offices.

Telephone and internet
The whole route has mobile phone (*handy* in German) coverage. Contact your network provider to ensure your phone is enabled for foreign use with the optimum price package. To make an international call dial the international access code of the country you are in (00 for the UK) followed by the dialling code for the country you wish to reach:
- Switzerland   +41
- Liechtenstein   +423
- Austria   +43

The infant Rhine descends from Lai da Tuma (Stage 1)

- Germany   +49
- France   +33
- The Netherlands +31

An increasing number of hotels, guest houses and hostels make internet access available to guests, often free but sometimes for a small fee.

Electricity
Voltage is 220v, 50HzAC. Plugs are mostly standard European two-pin round, but a third central earth pin is used in Switzerland. However, standard two-pin adaptors will work in all countries.

Clothing and personal items
Although the route is predominantly downhill, weight should be kept to a minimum. You will need clothes for cycling (shoes, socks, shorts or trousers, shirt, fleece, waterproofs) and clothes for evenings and days off. The best maxim is two of each, 'one to wear, one to wash'. Time of year makes a difference as you need more and warmer clothing in April/May and September/October. All of this clothing should be able to be washed en

Fully equipped cycle

route, and a small tube or bottle of travel wash is useful. A sun hat and sunglasses are essential, while gloves and a woolly hat are advisable, except in high summer.

In addition to your usual toiletries you will need sun cream and lip salve. You should take a simple first-aid kit. If staying in hostels you will need a towel and torch (your cycle light should suffice).

Cycle equipment

Everything you take needs to be carried on your cycle. If overnighting in accommodation, a pair of rear panniers should be sufficient to carry all your clothing and equipment, although if camping, you may also need front panniers. Panniers should be 100% watertight. If in doubt, pack everything inside a strong polythene lining bag. Rubble bags, obtainable from builders' merchants, are ideal for this purpose. A bar-bag is a useful way of carrying items you need to access quickly such as maps, sunglasses, camera, spare tubes, puncture kit and tools. A transparent map case attached to the top of your bar-bag is an ideal way of displaying maps and guide book.

Your cycle should be fitted with mudguards and a bell, and be capable of carrying water bottles, pump and lights. Many cyclists fit an odometer to measure distances. A basic tool-kit should consist of puncture repair kit, spanners, Allen keys, adjustable spanner, screwdriver, spoke key and chain

repair tool. The only spares worth carrying are two spare tubes (which are essential) and spare spokes. On a 1400km cycle ride, sometimes on dusty tracks, your chain will need regular lubrication and you should either carry a can of spray-lube or make regular visits to cycle shops. A good strong lock is advisable.

SAFETY AND EMERGENCIES

Weather

Most of the route is subject to a continental climate typified by warm, dry summers interspersed with short periods of heavy rain, and cold winters. However, the further you progress the greater the influence of Atlantic weather systems, with cooler summers, milder winters and more frequent but lighter periods of precipitation carried by a prevailing westerly wind. The first few stages are exposed to mountain weather with heavy winter snowfall. At lower altitudes this will have melted by April, but on the Oberalppass (Stage 1) snow may remain until May. Fresh snow may fall here at any time of year, although it is unusual in July and August. In the unlikely event that this stage is impassable, a train service connects Oberalppass with Disentis/Mustér, Ilanz and Chur.

Road safety

Throughout the route, cycling is on the right side of the road. Even if you have

AVERAGE TEMPERATURES (MAX/MIN DEGREES C)						
	Apr	May	Jun	Jul	Aug	Sep	Oct
Oberalppass	7/–4	14/0	17/3	19/5	19/5	14/1	11/–2
Basel	16/4	21/9	24/12	26/14	26/14	21/10	16/6
Köln	15/5	20/9	22/11	24/14	24/13	20/10	15/7
Rotterdam	14/5	18/8	20/11	22/13	23/13	19/11	15/8

AVERAGE RAINFALL (MM/RAINY DAYS)						
	Apr	May	Jun	Jul	Aug	Sep	Oct
Oberalppass	37/11	62/15	91/15	92/15	92/16	72/13	71/12
Basel	61/19	79/20	79/20	76/19	73/20	68/22	72/21
Köln	31/11	34/11	41/11	46/10	30/8	42/10	40/10
Rotterdam	46/20	70/17	85/18	97/20	101/20	137/22	115/23

*Contra-flow cycling allowed in
a one-way street*

never cycled on the right before you will quickly adapt, but roundabouts may prove challenging. You are most prone to mistakes when setting off in the morning. In France the general rule is to allow priority to traffic coming from your right, unless otherwise indicated. One-way streets often have signs permitting contra-flow cycling.

Much of the route is on dedicated cycle paths, although care is necessary as these are sometimes shared with pedestrians. Use your bell, politely, when approaching pedestrians from behind. In the Netherlands, where there are often cycle paths on both sides of the road, you should use the path on the right. If you do otherwise, you will soon generate frantic gesticulations from on-coming cyclists. Where you are required to cycle on the road there is usually a dedicated cycle lane, often in different coloured asphalt.

Many city and town centres have pedestrian-only zones. In Germany

39

such zones are only loosely enforced and you may find locals cycling within them – indeed many zones have signs allowing cycling. In the Netherlands, such restrictions are rigidly followed and you will receive angry looks and comments if you cycle in pedestrianised areas.

In none of the countries passed through is it compulsory to wear a cycle helmet, although their use is recommended. Modern lightweight helmets with improved ventilation have made wearing them more comfortable.

In Switzerland, cycling after drinking alcohol has the same 50mg/100ml limit as drink-driving (the UK drink-driving limit is 80mg/100ml). If you choose to cycle after drinking and

are caught you could be fined and banned from cycling, and driving, in Switzerland.

Emergencies

In the unlikely event of an accident, the standardised EU emergency phone number is 112. The entire route has mobile phone coverage. Provided you have a European Health Insurance Card (EHIC) issued by your home country, medical costs for EU citizens are covered under reciprocal health insurance agreements, although you may have to pay for an ambulance and claim the cost back through insurance. Although not EU countries, Switzerland and Liechtenstein are incorporated within these arrangements.

The red asphalt cycle lane of the Bodensee Radweg at Meersburg (Stage 5)

Insurance

Travel insurance policies usually cover you when cycle touring but they do not normally cover damage to, or theft of, your bicycle. If you have a household contents policy, this may cover cycle theft, but limits may be less than the real cost of your cycle. The Cycle Touring Club (CTC) offer a policy tailored for your needs when cycle touring (www.ctc.org.uk).

If you live in Switzerland and own a bicycle, you need to purchase an annual *velo vignette*, a registration sticker that includes compulsory third-party insurance. This is not a requirement for short-term visitors, but there have been proposals to extend this to all cyclists, which may be introduced during the lifetime of this guide.

ABOUT THIS GUIDE

Text and maps

There are 27 stages, each covered by a separate map drawn to a scale of approximately 1:333,000. At this scale it is not practical to cycle the route using only these maps, and you are advised to carry local, more detailed maps as well. However, sign-posting and waymarking are excellent throughout, and using these combined with the stage descriptions it should be possible to cycle much of the route without the expense or weight of carrying a large number of other maps. Beware, however, as the route described here does not always follow the waymarked route.

All places on the maps are shown in **bold** in the text. The abbreviation 'sp' in the text indicates a signpost. Distances shown are cumulative within each stage. Altitudes, where shown, are approximate, as the route may pass slightly above or below the point in each town where official altitude is calculated and an estimate has been made of altitude reached. For each city, town or village passed an indication is given of the facilities available (accommodation, refreshments, YH, camping, tourist office, cycle shop, station) when the guide was written. This list is neither exhaustive nor does it guarantee that establishments are still in business. No attempt has been made to list all such facilities as this would require another book the same size as this one. For a full listing of accommodation, contact local tourist offices or look online. Tourist offices in principal towns are listed in Appendix D.

All along the Rhine, large black-on-white number boards show kilometre distance from Konstanz Bridge where the river leaves Bodensee. These 'Rhine kilometres' are shown in principal places on the route maps.

While the route descriptions were accurate at the time of writing, things do change. Washouts from mountain streams can occur between Disentis/Mustér and Ilanz (Stage 1), sometimes requiring substantial deviations. On the Higher Rhine north of Karlsruhe

Rhine kilometre marker board

(Stage 13) and between Worms and Oppenheim (Stage 15); and on the Lower Rhine between Duisburg and Millingen an der Rijn (Stages 22 and 23), major works to create holding polders for flood water, to open up areas for sand and gravel extraction or to raise flood dykes have resulted in alterations to the route. Such works are expected to continue with other, as yet unknown, deviations to the route. Watch out for signs (often only in local languages) showing such alterations.

The Netherlands has a unique system of numbered knooppunten (waypoints). These are shown as 10 in stage descriptions and on the route maps.

Many alternative routes exist. Where these offer a reasonable variant (for instance are shorter, scenically superior, or have a better surface) they are mentioned in the text and shown on the maps. An indication of selected intermediate distances on variant routes is shown on the maps, calculated from the beginning of the relevant stage; note that the total distance for the stage given in the information box will need to be adjusted if the variant route is followed. For the journey across the Netherlands to the North Sea, two alternative routes are described after the main route.

Language
Place names, street names and points of interest are given in appropriate local languages. In German ß (known as an eszett) is expressed as double ss. Occasionally this results in triple sss appearing if ß is followed by s. Nouns and their descriptive adjectives are often run together to form longer words. Appendix B gives a glossary of words that might be encountered along the route.

STAGE 1
Oberalppass to Ilanz

Start	Oberalppass summit (2046m)
Finish	Ilanz square (699m)
Distance	52km
Signposting	R2

A fast descent on a well-surfaced minor alpine pass road through Surselva, passing a series of alpine villages, leads to the monastery town of Disentis/Mustér. From here, a mix of off-road tracks and quiet country lanes take you to Ilanz. Superb mountain scenery and high Alpine peaks abound. The Rhine evolves from a tiny mountain stream to a fast-flowing river over the course of this stage. The local language is Romansh, although German is spoken by all.

Rheinquelle

The official source of Vorderrhein (**Rheinquelle**) is an outflow from Lai da Tuma lake (2345m). This is high on the mountainside, S of Oberalppass, and can be reached by footpath (not accessible to cycles) from the pass summit (90min). Construction of Curnera dam and melting of Rhine glacier have greatly changed local hydrology and an alternate source, accessible to MTBs, exists at Lai Urlaun (2248m), 4.75km from the pass road. Touring bikes and hybrids can reach a group of chalets at Milex, from where it is a 75min walk. Short distance beyond this source is Swiss Alpine club refuge, Camona da Maighels (accommodation, refreshments).

From **Oberalppass** summit (2046m) (accommodation, refreshments, tourist office, station) follow road SE passing *gasthof* (guest house) R. After tourist office R (limited hours), where footpath leads across mountainside to **Rheinquelle**, road starts descending steeply around series of hairpin bends. ▶ On apex of ninth bend, 4wd track

Although Oberalppass is a quiet Alpine pass, it can become busy on summer weekends, particularly attracting many motorcyclists. Care should be taken as there is no dedicated cycle lane.

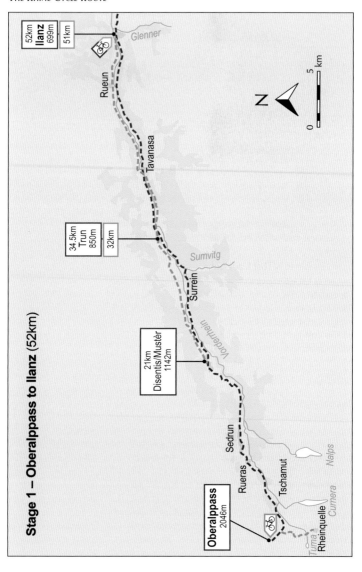

Stage 1 – Oberalppass to Ilanz (52km)

R (accessible to MTBs) leads uphill to alternative Rhine source at Lai Urlaun.

Tschamut, the first village on the Rhine

Road passes through tiny village of **Tschamut** (5.5km; 1645m) (accommodation, refreshments, station) and then continues above golf course at Selva, one of the highest in Europe. Levelling off, road crosses grassy plateau, passing in quick succession through villages of Dieni (accommodation, refreshments, station), **Rueras** (10.5km; 1405m) (accommodation, refreshments, camping, station), Camischolas (accommodation, refreshments, station) and **Sedrun** (12km; 1406m) (accommodation, refreshments, tourist office, station).

Visible across the valley from Sedrun is an intermediate shaft for boring the new 57km **Gotthard base tunnel**, a massive civil engineering project that is part of a planned high-speed rail link between Zürich and Milan. Drilling commenced in 1996, with opening of the link due in 2017. Original plans for the shaft at Sedrun to be used to access a station in the tunnel 800m below ground have been dropped.

Kloster St Martin at Disentis/Mustér

From Sedrun, road becomes busier as it resumes descending. After short tunnel and couple of hairpin bends, Disentis/Mustér, dominated by white façade of Kloster St Martin, comes into view. **Disentis/Mustér** (21km; 1142m) (accommodation, refreshments, camping, tourist office, cycle shop, station) is where you leave main road.

> Founded in 720, **Kloster St Martin** in Disentis is one of the oldest Benedictine abbeys in Switzerland. The current baroque edifice was completed in 1712. Plundered by French troops during the Napoleonic wars, the abbey barely survived the 19th century until restoration of Swiss religious houses in 1880 led to the founding of a secondary school. The community now includes 29 brothers.

On-road alternative
After Disentis/Mustér, route is mostly off-road, accessible to MTBs and hybrids. Going is not difficult and most touring bikes will have no problems, especially after Danis.

To bypass this section, use main road to Ilanz. Off-road and road routes intersect at Trun and Danis.

At T-junction in middle of Disentis/Mustér, turn R (Via Lucmagn) and after 150m L (Via dalla Staziun). Pass station R, and continue into Via Cavardiras, passing under railway and descending out of town.

> The whole way from Oberalppass to Chur, the route runs close to the railway line used by **Glacier Express** trains. Traversing the Swiss Alps from Zermatt in Valais to St Moritz and Davos in Graubünden, a service of four luxury tourist trains runs daily. Taking nearly 6hrs for 290km, this is the world's slowest 'express' train, but what it lacks in speed is made up for by spectacular scenery. There is no provision for cycles, but if you wish to traverse this line, there is an hourly local service that you can catch with your bike.

At T-junction, bear L onto cinder track and descend via series of hairpin bends towards river. On last hairpin

Old watermill at Disla

before bridge, bear L (do not cross bridge) onto cinder track parallel with river. Short stretch of asphalt leads through village of Disla, where old mill L has working overshot waterwheel. At T-junction, leave road bearing R onto undulating 4wd track cut into hillside. At end turn R onto cinder track and zigzag down through tiny hamlet of Madernal (25km; 975m) to cross Rhine for first time.

Continue through Pardomat, keeping straight ahead where track to Cavardiras turns sharply R, and after 200m, bear L on rough track into woods. Cross two small streams and after emerging from woods turn L downhill along cinder track. Turn R before river and climb past Resgia (accommodation, refreshments) on 4wd track that leads back to river opposite Cumpadials (accommodation, camping). Follow riverbank to reach asphalt road and turn R and immediately bear L along road through Reits to spread-out village of **Surrein** (30km; 895m) (accommodation).

At T-junction by Surrein church, turn R and after 75m fork R following road slightly uphill. Where asphalt ends, bear slightly L on cinder track into woods. Fork R across substantial girder bridge over Rein da Sumvitg river and turn L along 4wd track alongside washout. Continue for 2km on this track, which can be muddy when wet, bearing R along bank of Rhine. At end of woods, fork L on path alongside meadow. Turn L onto road and cross Rhine. After bridge bear R and head across meadows with Trun visible ahead and outdoor sculpture park R. Fork R, passing sports field R, and turn R at T-junction. ◄ Bear L, passing round behind timber yard, and continue on Via Ferrera across meadow. Bear L over bridge and level crossing to reach main road just E of **Trun** (34.5km; 850m).

Turn R for 75m along main road to filling station and fork L gently uphill to reach small village of Darvella. Turn R at T-junction back downhill. At bottom turn L past houses and barns. Where road ends, continue ahead on cycle track leading up to main road. Continue alongside main road for 150m and where road bears R to cross Rhine, turn L steeply uphill for 50m. Asphalt ends at farm where gravel track drops down ahead, cut into

To visit Trun (refreshments, camping, tourist office, station) turn L at T-junction before timber yard.

hillside above railway. This becomes 4wd track undulating alongside railway. Cross over railway and continue on ledge between the railway and Rhine to reach hydro-electric power station. Track becomes asphalt as it passes between dam R and substation L. Continue past generator hall R and alongside reservoir L. Fork R halfway along reservoir and drop down under railway bridge on 4wd track. Follow riverbank under two road bridges and immediately after second bridge turn sharply L uphill back under bridge. At top, turn R onto minor road between Danis and Tavanasa and bear R over Rhine. Turn L and continue through **Tavanasa** (40.5km; 788m).

Continue through village and bear L under railway bridge. Just before girder bridge over Rhine turn R onto dirt road. At three-way fork just before railway line, take middle fork along cinder track parallel with railway. Follow track as it bends R and L under railway before bearing away from railway following edge of forest R and meadows L for 5km, passing turn-off L to Waltensburg/Vuorx station. Re-enter forest and drop

Covered bridge leading to Rueun

Ilanz altstadt

down to riverbank, passing old covered wooden bridge that leads across Rhine to **Rueun** (47.5km) (accommodation, refreshments).

Continue S of river, mostly in trees, to road repair depot where tarred surface begins. At industrial estate, bear L parallel to Rhine on road behind factories. Pass under railway bridge and continue along riverbank entering Ilanz on Via Sorts with houses and allotments R. Bear R across level crossing and turn L (Giessli) with skyline of Ilanz *altstadt* (old town) R. Turn R (Via Centrala) to reach square in centre of **Ilanz** (52km; 699m) (accommodation, refreshments, tourist office, cycle shop, station).

> **Ilanz** (pop. 2350) is the first town on the Rhine. Points of interest in the altstadt (old town) include medieval walls, a reformed church (1518) and fine 15th and 16th-century houses.

STAGE 2
Ilanz to Chur

Start	Ilanz square (699m)
Finish	Chur station (585m)
Distance	35km
Signposting	R2

This is the only stage with significant ascent (250m). From Ilanz, the route climbs steadily following a minor country road to Versam, drops down, and then climbs again to a superb viewpoint high above the gorge of Ruinaulta. Descending to cross the river at the confluence of Vorderrhein and Hinterrhein in Reichenau/Tamins, an easy off-road route (accessible to touring cycles) is followed to the medieval city of Chur, capital of Graubünden canton.

From square in centre of **Ilanz**, follow Glennerstrasse E (sp Chur). At end of Ilanz, cross River Glenner, and join cycle track L, parallel to well-surfaced country road

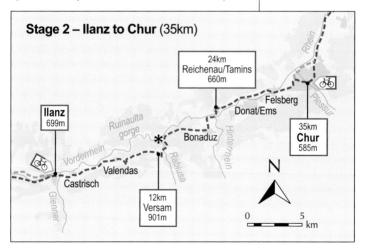

Stage 2 – Ilanz to Chur (35km)

ascending steadily to reach **Castrisch** (2km; 722m) where cycle track ends.

Turn R by fountain in centre of village and continue along road, descending gently for 1.5km, followed by steady ascent. First views of Ruinaulta canyon appear L, which will become more dramatic over next few kilometres. Continue climbing through **Valendas** (6.5km; 810m) (accommodation, refreshments) where there is a modern fountain.

Road descends slightly to cross sidestream, then begins steady ascent for 2km through hamlet of Carrera (855m) (camping), past turn R for Brun, to reach quarry L at top of pass. Descend gently to village of **Versam** (12km; 901m) (accommodation, refreshments), perched on side of gorge high above River Rabiusa.

Versam church perched above the Ruinaulta gorge

10,000 years ago the Flims rockslide brought 12 million cubic metres of limestone down into the Rhine Valley from the mountains lining its north side. This blocked the Vorderrhein and caused a lake to develop around what is now Ilanz. Over time,

Bridge over Rabiusa Gorge below Versam

pressure from this water forced a way through the blockage and a gorge was created as the river cut down through the debris to form **Ruinaulta canyon**. Lined by cliffs and fantastic rock formations several hundred metres high, the canyon is only accessible by foot, river or train with the Rhaetische Bahn railway running through the gorge. The river is popular for white-water rafting.

At end of Versam, bear L and descend steeply into gorge through series of hairpin bends. Cross bridge at bottom of hill (731m) and climb gently up other side. ▶

As road climbs, views of **Ruinaulta** improve, culminating with **viewpoint** (16.5km; 778m) set on bluff slightly above road L. From here you look directly down into gorge with Rhaetische Bahn railway following river far below. Road improves with long straight descent through woods. Cross level crossing, on line from St Moritz, and continue on Versamerstrasse into **Bonaduz** (20.5km; 655m) (accommodation, refreshments, cycle shop, station).

From Versam Bridge to Ruinaulta viewpoint, the road clings to the cliff face. It is narrow, poorly surfaced and has three tunnels, one with a bend in middle. Rock falls are common, so take care.

View from Ruinaulta viewpoint with a train in the gorge below

Do not go through centre of Bonaduz. 75m before road junction in village centre, turn L into Via Campagna, a small, easily missed, side street. This soon becomes country lane as it drops downhill past series of farms. After zigzag R and L, bear L through farm and over railway bridge. Turn R and follow railway until two hairpin bends take you down to riverbank L and under another railway bridge (Disentis line this time). Bear R, following railway again, and turn L onto quiet road. This leads to bridge over Vorderrhein and into **Reichenau** (23km; 592m) (Reichenau/Tamins: accommodation, refreshments, station).

Reichenau Bridge is the last bridge over Vorderrhein. Immediately downstream, visible from the bridge, is the **confluence of Hinterrhein and Vorderrhein**, and from here until the Netherlands, the river is known simply as the Rhine. In favourable weather conditions, the colour of the water flowing from each tributary differs, the two streams running side by side for several hundred metres before merging into one. This phenomenon is best seen from the bridge below the confluence, linking Reichenau with Reichenau/Tamins station.

After bridge, turn L into cobbled Reichenauer Strasse, which becomes asphalt as it climbs steeply towards Tamins. Near top of hill, follow road sharply R and after 100m turn L under main road, then immediately L steeply uphill (still called Reichenauer Strasse). At top, turn sharply R, climbing around bend on Afuris street into **Tamins** (24km; 660m).

Turn R at crossroads (Dorfplatz) and R again (Pradamaler Strasse), which winds out of village below church, becoming asphalt country lane on terrace cut into hillside. Drop steadily downhill, with shelters to protect against rock falls, and continue descending through meadows. Pass dam and hydro-electric station R, passing between woods L and river R, and then straight across meadows to **Felsberg** (29.5km; 572m) (refreshments, cycle shop, station).

Follow Taminserstrasse bearing R through village and turn R at crossroads into Burgstrasse. Cross river and motorway, then turn L off bridge between motorway and railway towards station. Just before station, bear L following cycle track alongside motorway. After 1km turn L, passing under motorway, and then R. As you approach

The confluence of the Vorderrhein (foreground) and Hinterrhein (right) at Reichenau

To bypass Chur, follow R2 continuing ahead from end of Rossbodenstrasse and loop round NW of town, between built-up area and river, to join Stage 3 on Reitnauerweg in Masans, just N of Chur.

outskirts of Chur, open area L is **army training ground**, from which gunfire and explosions may be heard. Bear L, cross entry road to army camp and turn R on parallel cinder cycle track. At end, cross road and turn L (Rossbodenstrasse) through industrial estate. At crossroads, turn R and follow Pulvermühlestrasse into **Chur**. ◀ Just before railway overbridge turn L (Segantinistrasse), then second R (Rheinstrasse). Fork L (Gartenstrasse) and continue into Gürtelstrasse to reach back entrance to Chur station (35km; 585m) (accommodation, refreshments, camping, tourist office, cycle shop, station).

Chur (pop. 37,000), first city on the Rhine and the oldest city in Switzerland, is the capital of Graubünden canton. The altstadt is a maze of medieval streets with many buildings listed by Swiss Heritage, including two cathedrals (Catholic and Protestant), three churches, four museums, four libraries and the old post office.

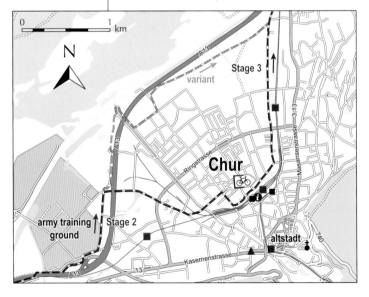

STAGE 3
Chur to Buchs

Start	Chur station (585m)
Finish	Buchs station (447m)
Distance	48km
Signposting	R2

After initially following the river closely as it turns north, the route climbs gently into the Maienfeld hills. This area of vineyards and alpine meadows is often called 'Heidiland', as it was the setting for Johanna Spyri's classic children's novel *Heidi*. Returning to the riverbank, the route passes Vaduz, capital of Liechtenstein, before ending at the railway junction town of Buchs. The Rhine flows through a deep valley, with high mountains to the east and west.

From rear of **Chur** station, follow Gürtelstrasse R and fork L (Wiesentalstrasse). Follow this for 1.5km, continuing into Reitnauerweg to rejoin R2. At roundabout, take second exit (Haldensteinstrasse), a moderately busy road with cycle lanes both sides. Just before Haldensteinstrasse crosses Rhine, turn R into Dornäuliweg, an asphalt cycle track beside river. Follow this past factory, then zigzag R and L to run parallel with railway for 2km. Bear L away from railway and continue on cinder track through woods with river L. Pass buildings materials depot and bear R, then L, continuing under road bridge. Bear L on road with series of factories, warehouses and power station R, with river behind trees L. After 1km pass under road bridge and bear R then L through car park in front of hotel and sports centre (accommodation, refreshments, station).

Continue past another building materials yard and bear L on cycle track parallel to railway. Bear L into woods to reach river, and continue on cinder track that eventually comes back to railway. Bear L and then fork R to follow railway under motorway bridge. Continue on road through industrial estate, bearing L between first

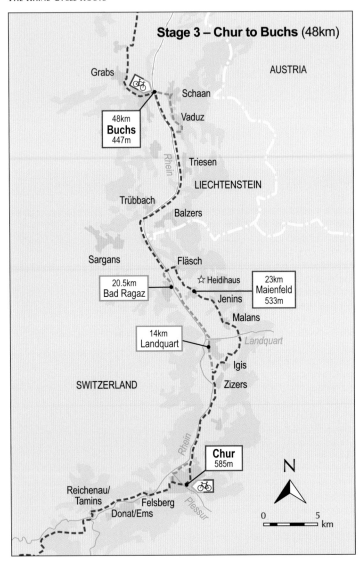

Stage 3 – Chur to Buchs (48km)

AUSTRIA

Grabs

Schaan

Vaduz

48km
Buchs
447m

Triesen

LIECHTENSTEIN

Trübbach

Balzers

Rhein

Sargans

Fläsch

20.5km
Bad Ragaz

☆ Heidihaus

23km
Maienfeld
533m

Jenins

Malans

14km
Landquart

Landquart

Igis

Zizers

SWITZERLAND

Rhein

Chur
585m

N

Reichenau/
Tamins

Felsberg

Donat/Ems

Plessur

0   5
km

and second units, then R onto quiet road that heads on through fields, with **Zizers** visible R across railway. After 800m, reach path junction R (11km; 528m). ▶

Turn R over railway and L at T-junction onto cycle track winding through fields. At barrier turn L across little bridge over stream. Continue ahead on cinder track with railway L to reach **Igis** station (12.5km) (cycle shop).

Turn R (Stationsstrasse) gently uphill, cross main road and continue uphill along residential street. At top of hill turn L into Luxgasse, a quiet country lane dropping down between fields. Fork R at bottom of hill and at crossroads turn R (Schalmans) with Schloss Marschlins castle (private residence) ahead. Turn L in front of castle gates and follow country lane winding NNW for nearly 2km. Turn L over stream and fork R under main road. Turn L and immediately R on cinder track into trees. At offset crossroads, continue ahead across Trattbrücke wooden arch bridge over River Landquart. Continue ahead over level crossing, then bear L on asphalt track that climbs between vineyards L and wooded hillside R. Cross stream and enter Malans on Prattigauerstrasse and continue along Sternengasse. This comes out at small square with fountain (statue of deer) in **Malans** (18km; 568m) (accommodation, refreshments, cycle shop, station).

Cross square into Heerengasse and continue past evangelical church L into Jeninserstrasse, climbing uphill out of village. Halfway uphill bear R, and at top follow Jeninserstrasse bearing L. Road continues past last houses of Malans L and contours across hillside with forest R. Descend to cross stream and climb following Malanserstrasse into **Jenins** (20.5km; 629m) (accommodation, refreshments).

Bear L following Unterdorfstrasse, through village centre past parish church R. Bear L, downhill (Jeninserstrasse) and continue through vineyards towards Maienfeld. Continue into Kruseckgasse, passing above centre of **Maienfeld** (23km; 533m) (accommodation, refreshments, tourist office, station). ▶

Alternative route bypassing Heidiland villages continues straight ahead. This follows railway through Landquart, then crosses motorway to follow riverbank for 5.5km, before crossing river and passing close to Bad Ragaz (5km shorter than main route).

To reach Maienfeld centre, turn L downhill at end of Kruseckgasse. Alternatively, to visit Heidihaus on hillside overlooking Maienfeld, turn R at end of Kruseckgasse and follow signs uphill.

The Heidihaus on the alm above Maienfeld

Heidi, from the famous novel by Johanna Spyri

One of the best-known Swiss novels, **Heidi**, a children's story written by Johanna Spyri, was published in 1880. It tells the tale of a young girl who, after her parents die, goes to live with her reclusive grandfather at his home on the *alm* (alpine meadow) above Maienfeld. The story has been adapted for film and TV around 20 times, the first in 1937 starring Shirley Temple. An animated version has made the story popular in Japan, and many Japanese tourists make their way to Heidihaus in Heididorf to visit the fictional setting for the book.

At T-junction, turn R and immediately L (Spitalgasse). Bear L and shortly turn R (Steigstrasse). Ascend gently past winery and fork L onto cycle track through vineyards. Bear R uphill on cycle track and bear L dropping downhill. Look out for sudden turn R (poorly signposted) onto 4wd track up through vines. Bear L at top and contour through vineyard, crossing stream and continuing ahead into Ob der Kircha street. Pass church L, and after 40m turn L (St Luzse street) to reach pretty centre of **Fläsch** (26km; 528m) (accommodation).

Fläsch church is famous for its colony of mouse-eared (*mausohren*) bats. Around 1000 of them roost in the baroque belfry every summer, although the number varies from year to year. A press-button-operated video screen on the outside wall provides live pictures of these creatures through an infrared camera.

Bear L (Hengert), and after 20m R into Krüzgass. Turn L (Unterdorf) and drop down bearing L. Turn R, and follow Augass, a concrete road descending to cross Rhine on new bridge (27km). ▶

At this point, direct route via Landquart rejoins. To visit spa town of Bad Ragaz, (accommodation, refreshments, camping, tourist office, cycle shop, station) continue straight ahead after bridge and follow signs.

Cycle track along the Rhine flood dyke north of Bad Ragaz

R2 continues along Swiss L bank of the river for further 13km directly to Buchs. Route described here makes brief excursion through Liechtenstein by crossing river and using R bank.

Turn R on asphalt track along top of Rhine flood dyke. Follow this for 6km as river bears R, passing border of Liechtenstein in mid-river, to reach cycle track bridge leading across river with Schloss Gutenberg castle on hill above **Balzers** (33km). ◄

Cross bridge and turn L along Liechtenstein side of river. Cycle along top of flood dyke following river as it bears L, passing under road bridge. Before next bridge, cycle track drops down L off flood dyke beside river to pass under bridge and reach newly restored covered wooden footbridge (41.5km). Vaduz can be seen R, with royal castle rising above.

Fürstentum Liechtenstein (Principality of Liechtenstein) is one of Europe's smallest countries (pop. 35,000), but is also the world's second richest in terms of GDP per capita. The country came into being in 1719 when Anton Florian of Liechtenstein (in Lower Austria) purchased Lordships of Schellenberg and Vaduz and combined them into one principality. The new 'prince' and his successors did not visit their country for 120 years. Indeed, the royal family continued living in Vienna until 1938, when the Anschluss (political union) between Germany and Austria threatened the position of the prince's Jewish wife.

Following the Second World War, Liechtenstein was in a poor financial position. However, a policy of low corporate taxation and banking confidentiality has attracted many companies and rich individuals, drawing huge investment into the principality. Liechtenstein today is in a customs union with Switzerland and uses Swiss francs. There are no immigration facilities at the border, but if you want your passport stamped the tourist office is happy to oblige.

To visit Vaduz

To visit **Vaduz** (457m) (accommodation, refreshments, camping, tourist office, cycle shop) turn R opposite

bridge, and immediately L (Binnendamm). Turn R (Kirchstrasse) and L at roundabout into Stadtle, the main pedestrianised street through town centre.

The royal castle at Vaduz

Either return same way, or continue through town following signs to **Schaan** (YH), where you turn L for Buchs.

Continue along dyke for 4.5km, passing national stadium and turn-off for Schaan (YH) R. Pass under railway bridge and road bridge. Soon after road bridge turn sharply back L and climb up to main road. Turn R to cross bridge on cycle lane. Continue ahead over motorway and bear R along Rheinstrasse, passing through station underpass and into **Buchs** (48km; 447m) (accommodation, refreshments, camping, tourist office, cycle shop, station).

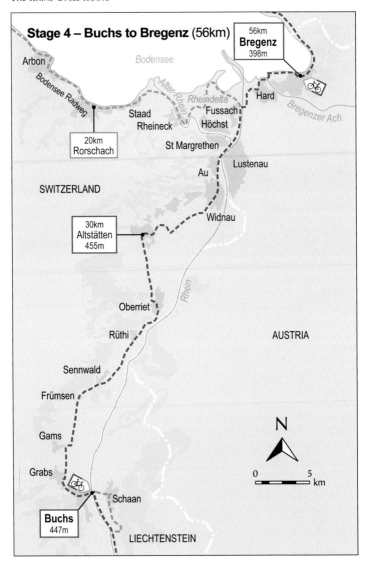

Stage 4 – Buchs to Bregenz (56km)

Arbon

Bodensee

Bodensee Radweg

Alter Rhein

Rheindelta

56km
Bregenz
398m

Hard

Bregenzer Ach

Staad
Rheineck

Fussach
Höchst

20km
Rorschach

St Margrethen

Au

Lustenau

SWITZERLAND

Widnau

30km
Altstätten
455m

Rhein

Oberriet

Rüthi

AUSTRIA

Sennwald

Frümsen

Gams

N

Grabs

0   5
km

Buchs
447m

Schaan

LIECHTENSTEIN

STAGE 4
Buchs to Bregenz

Start	Buchs station (447m)
Finish	Bregenz station (398m)
Distance	56km
Signposting	R2 Buchs–Fussach Bridge; BR Fussach Bridge–Bregenz

Although this is the last stage bounded by high mountains, the going is mainly level. Initially the route leads away from the river through agricultural land, often following irrigation canals, but the riverbank is regained at Au. Crossing into Austria and skirting the Rhein Delta, where the river enters Bodensee (Lake Constance), the stage ends at the lakeside resort of Bregenz.

From **Buchs** station follow Bahnhofstrasse (main shopping street) W. Continue into St Gallerstrasse. Bear R, passing pink church and continue into Werdenberg, with its castle on small hill overlooking lake and surrounded by old houses. ▶ Bear L at roundabout (Staatsstrasse) and continue gently uphill. Pass hospital L, then turn R (Fabrikstrasse) and follow round to L bypassing **Grabs** (3km) (accommodation, refreshments, cycle shop).

Turn R at mini-roundabout into Mühlbachstrasse and just before sports centre turn L (Werdenweg), which becomes quiet country lane (Bülsweg) between fields for 3km. Turn R onto Gams–Haag road, then L onto asphalt lane to continue between fields for further 4km. Turn R on Spengelgass into **Frümsen** (11km; 448m) (accommodation, refreshments).

Pass through village and continue on Holengass, rising over small ridge before dropping down towards **Sennwald** (453m) (refreshments). Just before village turn sharply R onto main St Gallen–Chur road and immediately L (Sägengass). After red-brick chimney stack fork L, and after 50m cross bridge and turn L on gravel track beside drainage canal. Continue for 2km, partly asphalt, to reach railway line. Bear L, parallel to railway and then

Although now swallowed up by Buchs, Werdenberg is regarded as the smallest town in Switzerland.

turn L and R to cross canal over sluice gate. Continue ahead under road bridge following canal across pleasant water meadows towards **Rüthi** (19km; 426m) (refreshments, station).

Follow Kanalstrasse, on W bank of canal, through Rüthi, with industrial units on opposite bank. Beyond village pass more industrial units, following the canal as it bears gently R. The next stretch of canal has been landscaped, providing wetland habitat for water birds. Continue on asphalt track through fields towards railway and pass small fortified tower on ridge L before Blatten. Pass under road bridge, continue past farm and at end turn L and R into Neudorfstrasse, leading into Oberriet. Turn L just before big factory R (Feldhofstrasse) and at T-junction bear L (Industriestrasse), with modern church in view. This brings you out on main road in **Oberriet** (23.5km; 421m) (accommodation, refreshments, cycle shop, station).

Turn R onto main road and after 75m L (Kellenstrasse), with fountain and statue of a mountaineer on corner. Continue slightly uphill out of village and just before road turns sharply L, turn R onto asphalt country lane. Follow this round past lake (visible through trees L) and bear R through arable fields. Cross a road and continue straight ahead (Erlenstrasse) crossing series of roads and drainage ditches, with Altstätten coming into view ahead. Enter town on Fleubenstrasse, gently uphill to a T-junction. Turn R (Eichbergerstrasse) to reach T-junction with main road. Turn L (Oberrieterstrasse) into **Altstätten** (30km; 445m) (accommodation, refreshments, tourist office, cycle shop, station). ◄

Turn R (Kriessenstrasse) and bear R into Bahnhofstrasse to rejoin R2, which has come through town centre. Cycle downhill to the railway, turn L in front of station and just after station, R across level crossing. After 100m, turn L (Bafflesstrasse), continuing through an industrial area where scrapyard R is graced with sculptured tree made from car parts. Continue past training stables and bear L over bridge into open country. Just before railway, bear R onto asphalt track bounded on L

To visit medieval Altstätten, turn L at next junction (Churerstrasse) following R2 signs to reach Marktgasse (main street) with many attractive buildings. Rejoin route by following Bahnhofstrasse out of town.

Cyclists in Marktgasse, Altstätten

by avenue of large oaks and follow this as it winds SE between fields for 1.5km. Cross small bridge and immediately turn L at crossroads onto rough gravel track. Follow this track NE beside drainage canal for 1.5km, then cross over to other side and continue on asphalt for further 2km. At T-junction, where canal enters larger watercourse, turn L, immediately cross a road and continue alongside wider canal (which you will follow for 6km). After 800m, turn R over canal and turn L following Lindenstrasse into **Widnau** (40km; 406m) (accommodation, refreshments, cycle shop, station).

Continue through Widnau, and after another street comes in R, leave road to follow cycle track along canal bank. Pass industrial units L and market gardens R, continuing past **Au** (Lustenau: accommodation, refreshments, tourist office, cycle shop, station).

Drop down and pass under motorway, turning L to follow motorway with Rhine 50m R. Soon after motorway bears away, pass under new railway bridge and climb up L onto Rhine dyke. Cross Swiss–Austrian border

Scrapyard at Altstätten

to reach path junction just before next road bridge. At this point you leave R2 (which bears L) dropping down briefly R under road bridge to continue following river to **Höchst** (accommodation, refreshments, tourist office, station). Drop down L to follow asphalt track below dyke. Continue, passing under main road between **Fussach** (accommodation, refreshments, camping, tourist office) and Bregenz, then turn immediately L and L again to cross over bridge on cycle lane. At this point you join Bodensee Radweg, or BR (48km; 398m).

South shore of Bodensee
Lake Constance (Bodensee) can be circumnavigated either via S (Swiss) shore or N (Austrian–German) shore. R2 follows S shore, passing through the primarily resort towns of Rorschach and Romanshorn en route to Konstanz. While this is shorter (58km to Konstanz compared to 69km plus ferry via N shore), it is less attractive and less interesting than N route through Bregenz, Lindau, Friedrichshafen and Meersburg. This guide describes as the main route the N route through Austria and Germany.

The Rhein Delta, with the milky water of the Rhine (left) entering Bodensee

See map at Stage 5.

The S route, which runs close to lake for most of the way, is well signposted throughout, as both R2 and BR. The route leaves main route at Fussach Bridge and goes through **Rheineck**, **Rorshach** and **Arbon** to reach **Romanshorn** after 36km. ◄ It then goes through **Uttwil** and **Landschlacht** (49.5km) to arrive at **Kreuzlingen** and Swiss–German border (58.5km)

Continue over two smaller canals and turn immediately L. Follow canal N, passing Mockenstrasse R and after 1.3km bear R on cinder track between trees. Follow this round side of small lagoon. Cross two bridges, pass skatepark R and bear L on asphalt track, turning R in front of small marina to reach road. Turn L (Uferstrasse), pass Hard church R and bear L into Kohlplatzstrasse in **Hard** (51km) (accommodation, refreshments, YH, camping, tourist office, cycle shop, station).

Pass series of marinas and boatyards L and continue into Hafenstrasse. At end, turn R on asphalt track along flood dyke. At crossroads turn L onto new concrete bridge over Bregenzer Ach river. Turn L onto quiet road, and where this turns R, continue ahead for 200m past car park. Bear R, passing cafe L and follow winding cinder cycle track through woods with parallel footpath. This becomes asphalt, passes campsite R, and crosses small humpback bridge. Continue past playing fields R and Bregenz sailing club. Cross another small bridge, bear L and R past car park R. Pass under archway between sports stadium R and sports centre L, then turn L and R to circle football pitch. Turn sharply L, passing car park for open air theatre, Mercure hotel and casino (all L) and cut across car park R to reach back entrance to **Bregenz** station (56km; 398m) (accommodation, refreshments, camping, tourist office, cycle shop, station).

Every summer **Bregenz** (pop. 28,000) plays host to Festspiele, a major music and arts festival. The centrepiece is a massive outdoor opera performance on the Seebühne, a unique floating stage on the edge of Bodensee with on-shore seating for 7000

spectators. Performances are drawn from the popular operatic repertoire, and feature innovative staging making use of the lake. Recent performances have included *Aida*, *Tosca* and *Il Trovatore*. The season runs from late July until early September, with tickets available from the box office or tourist office. Prices range from €25 to over €100. Should rain intervene and the performance be cancelled, those with higher-priced seats get to see an indoor adaptation in the Festspielhaus, while holders of the cheaper tickets get their money back.

The Seebühne festival stage in Bregenz

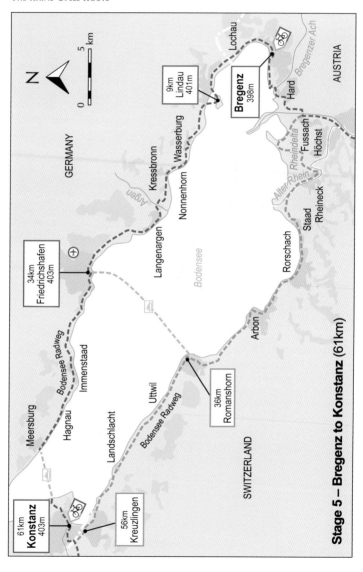

Stage 5 – Bregenz to Konstanz (61km)

STAGE 5
Bregenz to Konstanz

Start	Bregenz station (398m)
Finish	Konstanz Bridge (403km)
Distance	57km (plus 4km ferry)
Signposting	BR and D8

This stage circles around the north side of Bodensee, sometimes on the lakeshore but more often gently undulating a short distance inland. The route passes through a number of resort towns and villages, including the picturesque medieval port town of Lindau and small industrial city of Friedrichshafen, home of the Zeppelin airship. From Meersburg, a car ferry is used to cross Bodensee to Konstanz. This is a productive fruit growing area, with vineyards passed later.

The Bodensee Radweg is one of the most popular German cycling routes, and you will encounter a steady stream of cyclists, young and old. Accommodation is plentiful, but nevertheless you should consider booking ahead, especially during weekends in high season. The complete circuit of the lake, including its various arms, takes four to five days.

From back of **Bregenz** station, take cycle track NE, between railway R and lakeside gardens L. Pass harbour L and continue out of Bregenz on dual-use (pedestrian/cycle) track between railway and lakeshore. Continue past Strandbad Lochau private bathing area and follow track bearing L around lakeshore side of Seehotel. Return to railway and continue past **Lochau** station (3.5km) before crossing bridge over river marking Austro–German border (accommodation, refreshments, camping, tourist office, station).

Continue past allotments R and campsite L following the railway, and bear L (Eichwaldstrasse). Pass Villa Leuchtenberg L and a popular bathing area. Just after road turns R towards railway bridge, turn L into Ladestrasse, a quiet road between trees. Pass railway goods depot R, and bear L at T-junction beside level crossing into Bregenzer

Entrance to Lindau harbour

To visit Lindau centre continue straight ahead then fork R along Schmiedgasse into Marktplatz. From here Cramergasse and Maximilianstrasse lead through old town towards harbour. Return to route by taking Dammsteggasse (N from Maximilianstrasse, R of post office) continuing on cycle track beside railway.

Strasse, a busy road with cycle lanes. Bear L at roundabout, and cross bridge to reach another roundabout on **Lindau** island (9km; 401m) (accommodation, refreshments, YH, camping, tourist office, cycle shop, station). ◄

Although technically an island, the enchanting medieval town of **Lindau** (pop. 25,000) is connected to the mainland by a causeway and a bridge. A self-governing free city until 1802, it grew rich due to its position on the Nuremburg to Italy trading route. The old town centre of cobbled streets and alleyways contains many spectacular edifices including the *rathaus* (town hall). Lindau's most famous landmark is its harbour entrance, flanked by a carved lion on one side and lighthouse on the other. The town is a very popular tourist destination.

Turn R, and continue on Zwanzigerstrasse skirting the old town. Just before road starts to rise over railway bridge, bear R and immediately L (Sina-Kinkelin-Platz). Turn R onto cycle track coming from Lindau centre and continue over causeway with railway L. At T-junction turn L over level crossing and follow Lotzbeckweg along lakeshore. Continue along Giebelbachstrasse and turn L (Schachener Strasse), which you follow for 2km winding through Bad Schachen. At end of village bear R (Reutenerstrasse) passing orchards and fork L through Reutenen. Continue through orchards, past swimming complex L, and turn L to follow Höhenstrasse past campsite L into **Wasserburg** (14.5km) (accommodation, refreshments, camping, tourist office, station).

Turn L at cobbled village square (Lindenplatz) into Halbinselstrasse, winding down through village towards lakeshore. At T-junction, turn R into Mooslachenstrasse. ▶ Fork L past car park and bear L on multi-use gravel path continuing into Wasserburger Strasse. Bear L at T-junction (Conrad-Forster-Strasse) and follow this as it winds through **Nonnenhorn** (17.5km) (accommodation, refreshments, camping, tourist office, cycle shop, station).

Turn L to reach Wasserburg harbour, parish church of St George and Schloss Hotel.

At staggered crossroads turn L (Mauthausstrasse) and R (Uferstrasse). Continue out of village parallel to lake through orchards and continue along Nonnenhornerstrasse into **Kressbronn** (19km) (accommodation, refreshments, camping, tourist office, cycle shop, station).

In village centre turn L into Bodanstrasse and follow this, bearing R parallel to lakeshore past boatyard and marina L. Continue on cycle track (L of road) and where road bears R, continue ahead on gravel track through fields into hamlet of Tunau. Turn L on asphalt track and bear R at fork to pass through Schnaidt campsite. Continue ahead at roundabout and at end of campsite, where road bears L, continue ahead on gravel track through orchards. Turn L at T-junction (Tunauerweg) into Gohren and L at next T-junction into main road (Langenargener Strasse). Proceed on cycle track parallel to road, crossing River Argen on old suspension bridge beside modern road bridge. Turn L (Bleichweg) and bear R (Obere Seestrasse) alongside lakeside gardens into **Langenargen** (25km) (accommodation, refreshments, tourist office, cycle shop, station).

Bear R and immediately L (Schulstrasse), Continue along cobbled Marktplatz, past monastery and St Martins church L, and ahead into Untere Seestrasse, which is followed parallel to lakeshore bearing L at end of Langenargen. Turn R (Schussenweg) and after 200m L onto asphalt track winding past sewerage works. Turn L just before level crossing onto gravel cycle track parallel to railway. Cross river on suspension bridge, then turn L at T-junction and immediately R onto another gravel track winding through orchards. Pass Eriskirch station R and continue parallel to railway for 3km crossing two roads and passing Kretzen L, where surface becomes asphalt. Bear R and L at T-junction into Seewiesenstrasse and continue under road bridge. Turn immediately L (Lindauerstrasse) and bear R to join main road. Pass YH R, cross river bridge and continue on cycle lane beside Eckenerstrasse. At crossroads, turn L (Romanshorner Platz). Bear R, past ferry entrance on L, into bus station and turn L passing behind bus parking bays with Hafenbahnhof station R. Turn R between station and Zeppelin Museum and continue on cobbled Karlstrasse through **Friedrichshafen** (34km; 403m) (accommodation, refreshments, YH, camping, tourist office, cycle shop, station).

In 1898 Count Ferdinand von Zeppelin founded a company producing dirigible rigid-frame **Zeppelin airships** from a floating hangar at Friedrichshafen (pop. 59,000). During the First World War, airships were constructed for wartime service, mostly for naval observation, but also for bombing. Post-war restrictions on German military activities led the company to concentrate on civilian craft, including the Graf Zeppelin, which circumnavigated the globe and was used for regular transatlantic services to Brazil. Recognising the danger of using hydrogen, the gigantic Hindenburg was designed to use helium. However, an American embargo prevented Germany from obtaining enough helium and Hindenburg was filled with hydrogen – disastrous consequences ensued when she caught fire

Zeppelin-Haus and statue, Friedrichshafen

arriving in New York (1937). At the beginning of the Second World War, remaining airships were grounded and eventually broken up to provide aluminium for aeroplane manufacture.

In addition to telling the Zeppelin story, the centrepiece of the Zeppelin Museum in Friedrichshafen is a reconstructed section of the Hindenburg, complete with cabins and lounges. Count von Zeppelin is commemorated around Friedrichshafen with a monument, statue and conference hall named in his honour. However, the story is not over, and since the 1990s a new company has been building NT (new technology) Zeppelins in Friedrichshafen. These can often be seen in the skies around Bodensee.

Follow Karlstrasse bearing R gently uphill, with lakeside gardens L. Turn L (Friedrichstrasse) alongside the gardens, passing Zeppelin monument L. Turn L at end of gardens towards Zeppelinhaus and immediately fork R (Klosterstrasse). Just after entrance to monastery turn R up residential street (Schlossstrasse) and L before railway bridge (Schmidstrasse). Continue out of Friedrichshafen parallel with railway R. Turn L downhill at T-junction (Schwanenweg), R at next T-junction (Möwenstrasse) and R at crossroads (Reiherweg). Pass under railway bridge and bear R into underpass beneath main road. Turn L on dual-use cycle/pedestrian track beside road (Zeppelinstrasse), following this for 5km over bridge crossing railway and local road then through Fischbach (accommodation, refreshments, camping), where road becomes Meersburger Strasse. Pass between industrial units L and R, and follow service road R to just before it drops down to pass under main road. Bear R on cycle track uphill and at top cross side road and turn L, then bear R to rejoin cycle track alongside main road. Continue for 200m, then drop down R and bear back L under main road. Turn R (Friedrichshafener Strasse) and continue along Hauptstrasse into **Immenstaad** (44.5km) (accommodation, refreshments, camping, tourist office, cycle shop).

Continue following main road through Immenstaad and just before this reaches the bypass, cross the road onto service road L parallel with bypass (St-Vinzenz-Pallotti-Weg). Pass winery surrounded by vineyards R and continue on cycle track alongside road. This becomes service road for campsite at Schloss Kirchberg and just before it ends, turn L and R (Strandbadstrasse) through campsite. Continue through orchards and vineyards into **Hagnau** (48.5km) (accommodation, refreshments, camping, tourist office).

Turn L (Dr.-Fritz-Zimmerman-Strasse) and pass under archway beneath town hall. Turn R through very pretty part of Hagnau onto Seestrasse. Pass gardens and small quay L and continue along lakeshore road (Meersburger Strasse), which becomes cycle track once past village. Stay on lakeshore track for 3km, passing vineyards and marinas, which becomes road (Uferpromenade) as it nears Meersburg. Pass below large winery on ridge R and enter medieval **Meersburg** on Unterstadtstrasse (52.5km) (accommodation, refreshments, tourist office).

Meersburg (pop. 5600) is really two towns in one, lakeside Innenstadt with its colourful houses, medieval gateway and harbour; and Oberstadt on vine-covered hillside with two castles and many viewpoints. Altes Burg (old castle) is claimed to be the oldest inhabited castle in Germany, originating with the seventh-century Merovingian dynasty; Neues Schloss (new castle) is a baroque palace built for the prince-bishop of Konstanz (completed in 1760). Near to the new castle is the state winery. A ferry can be caught to the garden island of Mainau, but bicycles are not carried as they are forbidden on Mainau.

Meersburg harbour, with Neues Schloss on the hill above

Continue through archway under clock tower, with castle above R. After 100m, bear L on red asphalt cycle track, dropping down along the lakeshore to ferry terminal. Take car ferry (frequent 24-hour service) to **Staad** (accommodation, refreshments, YH, camping).

From ferry terminal continue ahead uphill (Schiffstrasse). At top of hill bear L at traffic lights

To reach Konstanz YH, turn R at the traffic lights into Mainaustrasse and second R (Zur Allmannshöhe).

(Mainaustrasse) and follow this, winding downhill on cycle track beside road. ◀ At bottom of hill bear L under railway bridge, then follow cycle track bearing slightly R away from road and L through underpass. Turn R and circle up R onto Konstanz Bridge and follow cycle track across Rhine into **Konstanz** (57km plus 4km ferry; 403m) (accommodation, refreshments, tourist office, cycle shop, station).

To visit centre of Konstanz
Route follows riverbank, bypassing Konstanz. To visit city centre, drop down R after crossing river and follow sign-posted cycle route under road into old town.

Konstanz Bridge, zero point for Rhine kilometres, with the cathedral in the distance

The bishopric of **Konstanz** (pop. 85,000) was established in AD585 and by the Middle Ages the city had developed into one of Europe's most important religious centres. The Council of Konstanz (1414–1418), the only papal conclave held north of the Alps, elected Pope Martin V and ended the

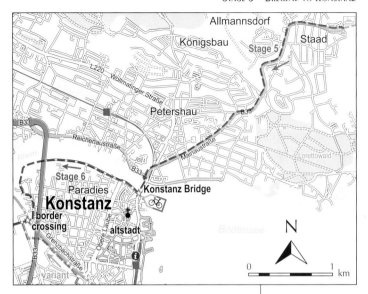

schism between Avignon and Roman popes, while Jan Hus (founder of the Czech Protestant church) was condemned and burnt at the stake for heresy. Important buildings include the *münster* (cathedral), three original towers from the old city wall and Konzilgebäude, where the council took place.

Leaving Konstanz, either retrace your steps or follow cycle route signs to Switzerland along Gottlieberstrasse and over motorway bridge to rejoin main route at German–Swiss **border crossing**.

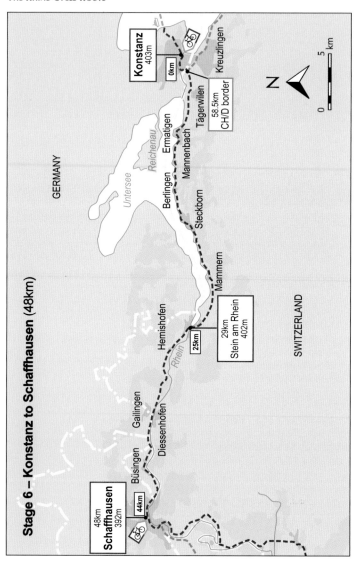

Stage 6 – Konstanz to Schaffhausen (48km)

Konstanz 403m
0km

Kreuzlingen

Tägerwilen

58.5km CH/D border

GERMANY

Reichenau

Untersee

Ermatigen
Mannenbach
Berlingen
Steckborn

Mammem

Hemishofen

25km

29km Stein am Rhein 402m

Rhein

SWITZERLAND

Gailingen

Büsingen

Diessenhofen

48km Schaffhausen 392m
44km

N

0   5
km

STAGE 6
Konstanz to Schaffhausen

Start	Konstanz Bridge (403m)
Finish	Schaffhausen Bridge (392m)
Distance	48km
Signposting	R2

Initially following the south (Swiss) shore of the Untersee arm of Bodensee, this stage of the route crosses the river at the walled town of Stein am Rhein to continue along the north side of the Rhine. Two short sections of Germany are crossed, including the enclave of Büsingen, before you reach the Swiss city of Schaffhausen. Forested hills, occasionally reaching the river, line the valley.

Konstanz and Schaffhausen (and many piers between) are connected by a regular (two-hourly) boat service that takes cycles.

From S side of **Konstanz Bridge**, follow cycle track W beside Rheinsteig. Where main road bears L, continue ahead on quiet road beside river (Webersteig which becomes Wintersteig). Pass under motorway and bear L following lakeside track. Continue into Fischenzstrasse, bearing L, and fork R just in front St Martin's Kapelle into cobbled Griesseggstrasse. Bear R onto asphalt and at end turn R (Gottlieber Strasse) to reach Swiss–German **border post**.

At this point route rejoins R2. Continue ahead into open country on cycle track L parallel to Konstanzerstrasse. At junction with main road, bear R on cycle track parallel with road, passing **Tägerwilen** L, and where road drops down to pass under railway, fork R and follow road bearing R towards Gottlieben. After 200m, turn L onto gravel track between fields (Riedstrasse). Continue for 3.5km, zigzagging L and R at offset track junction by Triboltingen station and following railway. Turn R at road junction by level crossing and L at T-junction (Hornstrasse) to reach centre of **Ermatingen** (8.5km) (accommodation, refreshments, tourist office, station).

The Rathaus at Steckborn

Continue over crossroads (Heimgartenstrasse), turn L at T-junction (Untere Seestrasse) and fork R onto quiet residential street (Westerfeldstrasse) with lake behind houses R. Where asphalt bears L, continue R on gravel track out of village, with railway L and sports field R. After 1km, cross railway at second level crossing, turning R along the other side to soon reach main road. Follow cycle track bedside road to reach **Mannenbach** (11.5km) (accommodation, refreshments, station).

Just beyond station fork R onto cycle track, cross railway R at level crossing and follow a road L looping the village and recrossing railway at next crossing. Turn immediately R (Stadtgraben), parallel with railway on cycle track between railway R and main road L. This soon becomes cycle track alongside road, crossing railway and continuing on Seestrasse along lakeshore through pretty village of **Berlingen** (14km) (accommodation, refreshments, tourist office, station).

Beyond the village, cycle track continues along lakeshore, eventually becoming cycle lane alongside main road to reach **Steckborn** (17km) (accommodation, refreshments, camping, tourist office, station).

Continue through town and bear R at roundabout along main road (Seestrasse) up a slight rise. At top, turn L between factories and cross railway on level crossing. After 100m turn R at T-junction (Weierstrasse), then fork R and immediately R again (Bollanderstrasse). Turn L before railway underbridge (Glariseggerweg) and follow this into open country as it becomes cycle track parallel to railway. Join main road and continue ahead on cycle track with road R, past Schloss Glarisegg conference centre L. Drop down, turning R to pass under road and bearing L to continue following road. Continue alongside railway R for 3km and rejoin road at T-junction, bearing R over level crossing and L on Hauptstrasse into **Mammern** (23km) (accommodation, refreshments, camping, tourist office, station).

Turn L uphill in village centre (Liebenfelsstrasse). After 80m turn R before first level crossing (Bahnhofstrasse), then L over second level crossing and immediately R (Huebackerstrasse) past station, parallel to railway. Continue through orchards and after 1.5km turn steeply uphill L for 50m. Turn R back downhill, and soon L and R to contour across hillside. Zigzag L and R around factory, then R and immediately L. Turn R at T-junction (Bahnhofstrasse) past Eschenz station R, then L and R at offset crossroads into Wasenstrasse. Bear R and L, then continue ahead on cycle track following railway out of village. Cross two tracks, then turn L and R into Gewerberstrasse, continuing alongside railway. Turn R across level crossing and L at roundabout. Fork immediately R downhill (Charregass) and cross Rhine. Continue up other side of river, bearing L in front of Rathaus into centre of **Stein am Rhein** (29km; 402m) (accommodation, refreshments, YH, camping, tourist office, cycle shop, station).

> **Stein am Rhein** (pop. 3200), situated at the western end of Untersee where Bodensee empties into the Rhine, is one of the best-preserved medieval towns in Switzerland. Rathausplatz and Understadt (main street) are pedestrianised streets lined with highly frescoed buildings, many of them Swiss Heritage listed. The wood-framed buildings of St Georgen Abbey (now a museum) perch on the riverbank, while Hohenklingen Castle lies 200m above town.

Continue across cobbled Rathausplatz and downhill along Understadt, lined with attractive medieval houses. Pass under Untertor arch through city walls, and continue ahead on main road (Hemishoferstrasse). Opposite end of riverside gardens, turn R uphill (Schwemmgraben) and after 50m L (Niderfeld-Strasse) leading to asphalt track parallel to main road. Pass YH L, then cross road by underpass and continue between road and river, passing under two bridges into **Hemishofen** (32km) (accommodation, refreshments).

In middle of village turn L downhill (Dorfstrasse), bearing R after 50m through old part of village. Continue on concrete cycle track through arable fields. ◀ Path

Although north of the Rhine, the bowl to the right encircled by wooded hills is part of Switzerland, while Rosenegg Castle visible in the distance is in Germany.

becomes asphalt and forks R uphill towards trees. At next fork L, gravel track winds steeply into forest, crossing Swiss–German border. Passing little hut at summit (449m), descend through barrier out of forest and continue on asphalt track, firstly through fields and then along riverbank to arrive at covered bridge between **Diessenhofen** in Switzerland (opposite) and **Gailingen** in Germany (38.5km) (accommodation, refreshments, tourist office). ▸

Stein am Rhein, one of the best-preserved medieval towns in Switzerland

Continue along road following river, bearing R for short distance uphill. At top fork L on gravel path with both German and Swiss signs. After 1.2km the path crosses German–Swiss border. Bear L at farm and re-enter Germany (this time into enclave of Büsingen) by a campsite. Emerging from trees, Büsingen church is visible on hilltop R. Turn L at T-junction and follow cycle lane on main road through **Büsingen** (43.5km) (accommodation, refreshments, tourist office).

Gailingen can be reached by turning R, following road steeply uphill for 1km.

Büsingen (pop. 1400) has been a German enclave surrounded by Swiss territory since the early 19th century. Despite a 96% vote in 1918 to become part of Switzerland, the village remained German as the Swiss had no suitable territory to exchange. Citizens with over 10 years' residence have honorary Swiss citizenship. Büsingen is in a customs union with Switzerland and although the official currency is the Euro, Swiss francs are commonly used. Although children may attend secondary school in either country, 70% choose Switzerland. The village has both German and Swiss postcodes and telephone dialling codes.

At end of village, cycle track appears between road and river for 1km, before reverting to cycle lane on road, which continues over German–Swiss border to enter Schaffhausen by Rheinhaldenstrasse. **Munot Fortress** is visible on hill ahead. Just as older buildings start to appear, cycle lane ends and cycle track starts L of road. This goes round car park before forking L under

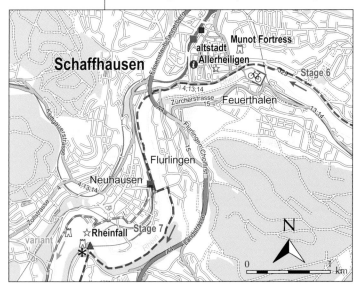

building and railway bridge. Continue along Rheinquai, passing boat landing stages and under road bridge into **Schaffhausen** (48km; 392m) (accommodation, refreshments, YH, camping, tourist office, cycle shop, station). ▶

Schaffhausen, with the Munot Fortress overlooking the Rhine

To visit Schaffhausen, which sits on hill N of river, turn R after bridge, cross main road and follow signs to centre.

Schaffhausen (pop. 34,600) grew up as a portage station where goods were unloaded to be carried around the Rhein Falls. This attracted merchants and traders and the pedestrianised old town contains many highly decorated guild and merchant houses in both the Gothic and baroque style. Other important buildings include Allerheiligen Benedictine Abbey below the old town and Munot Fortress on the adjoining hilltop, where a curfew bell is sounded nightly at 2100.

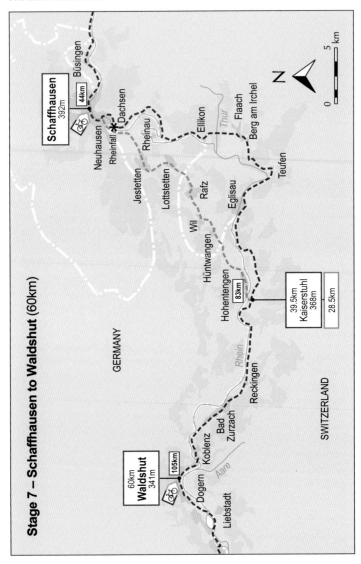

Stage 7 – Schaffhausen to Waldshut (60km)

STAGE 7
Schaffhausen to Waldshut

Start	Schaffhausen Bridge (392m)
Finish	Waldshut town hall (341m)
Distance	60km (49km via Lottstetten, Germany)
Signposting	R2 (Swiss side of river), D8 (German side of river)

Following the south (Swiss) side of the Rhine, you pass continental Europe's largest waterfall then follow the river as it cuts its way through a range of wooded hills. The undulating route is mostly on a small plateau overlooking the river in a gorge below, occasionally dropping down to the riverbank. The scenery is mainly agricultural, although there are a number of cement works. An alternative, direct route exists on the north (German) side of the river. This is 11km shorter than the main route, and the cumulative distances given in the route description should be adjusted accordingly.

From **Schaffhausen Bridge**, follow cycle track along N bank of Rhine, between main road (Rheinuferstrasse) and river. Pass hydro-electric station L and continue along riverbank, dropping down to pass under two bridges. 200m after second bridge ignore pedestrian path continuing ahead and turn R on cycle track between buildings. Turn L on quiet road (Rheinweg) and follow this as it leads to gravel track along riverbank. At next bridge in **Neuhausen** (2.5km) there is choice of routes.

Route north of river
By turning sharply back R just before bridge and passing under railway you can follow D8, leading behind factories to N (German) side of Rheinfall. D8 then continues SW, cutting across the plateau through **Lottstetten** (9.5km) directly to Hohentengen and Kaiserstuhl (28.5km). This saves 11km, but misses the best scenery of the whole stage.

The Rheinfall

Turn L over bridge (Neuhauserstrasse) and R into Lächenstrasse, a quiet residential road. At end continue on gravel track along riverbank, undulating through woods then climbing steeply to Schloss Laufen (YH) overlooking **Rheinfall** (4.5km) (refreshments, YH, station).

With a width of 150m and drop of 23m, **Rheinfall**, continental Europe's largest waterfall by volume of water, was formed during the last ice age (14,000–17,000 years ago) when the Rhine changed course to flow over a hard limestone sill. The falls can be seen and visited from both sides of the river. Tickets to visit the falls from Schloss Laufen (by stairs or lift) can be purchased at the visitors' centre by the car park. Frequent boats cross the river below the falls, linking Laufen with Schloss Wörth castle, from where other boats make spray-drenched excursions beneath the falls themselves. A landing can be made on Rheinfallfelsen, a rock in the middle of the falls with spectacular views. Over the course of many years there have been plans to bypass Rheinfall with locks for navigation and hydro-electric dams, but these have all been rejected.

Leave Schloss Laufen by road between main car park L and cemetery R. Bear R on quiet country road and continue through **Dachsen** (5.5km) (accommodation, refreshments, cycle shop, station).

At end of village, take middle of three roads (Benkemerstrasse) uphill, and after 150m bear R into Marthalerstrasse. Continue across agricultural plateau with Rhine in wooded gorge R, then through woods and under railway to T-junction with main road. Bear R (Poststrasse), pass psychiatric hospital L to reach sharp bend L where road R leads to **Rheinau** (11.5km; 392m). ▶

On an island in a bend of river below Rheinau is **Kloster Rheinau** (Rheinau Abbey). The original Romanesque basilica was abandoned during the 16th-century Protestant reformation, but was later re-established as a Benedictine monastery and rebuilt in the baroque style in 1744. It closed in 1862 and became a hospital and nursing clinic, latterly for psychiatric patients. Closed again in 2000, the building currently stands empty.

To visit Rheinau (1km) (accommodation, refreshments, tourist office), turn R through upper part of village then drop down to older part beside bridge to abbey.

Rheinau Abbey

Turn sharply L (Ellikonerstrasse), and 250m beyond end of village R onto asphalt track winding down through woods towards river. Where asphalt turns sharply R, bear L on gravel track parallel to river. At fork where footpath continues along riverbank, bear L on 4wd track (Reutenenweg) through woods for 2km initially level, then ascending and finally level again. Bear L out of woods and turn R onto main road downhill past **Ellikon** (15.5km) (accommodation, refreshments).

Continue downhill through woods, cross River Thur and straight ahead across agricultural plateau with wooded ridge visible ahead. Where road bears L, continue ahead on gravel track towards **Flaach** (19km; 362m) (accommodation, refreshments, camping, cycle shop).

Fork R past barn into village and fork R (Platte) between houses, then ahead into Moosstrasse. Turn L at T-junction, then fork L and continue ahead over main road climbing past church R on Bergstrasse. Continue steadily uphill, bearing L into pretty village of **Berg am Irchel** (20km; 410m) (refreshments).

Turn R (Dorfstrasse), continuing uphill through fields. Crest summit (450m) and descend through woods

A beautiful stretch of river at Tössegg

round series of hairpin bends to **Teufen** (25km; 420m) (refreshments).

At end of village, turn R steeply downhill on quiet country road through vineyards, to hamlet of Tössegg in beautiful setting overlooking river bend (refreshments). Turn L at river, cross small bridge over sidestream and bear R on gravel track along riverbank. Climb away from river following Waldheimstrasse through pretty Tössrieden and bear R on quiet road (Rhihaldenstrasse) towards Eglisau. Just before village, turn L uphill (Roggenfarstrasse), bear R, then straight over at crossroads. At main road, turn R and immediately L uphill (Bahnstrasse), passing **Eglisau** station L (29.5km; 370m) (accommodation, refreshments, tourist office, cycle shop, station).

Follow road R and turn L at T-junction to pass under railway viaduct and head out of village on Rheinsfelderstrasse. You are now on wide cultivated shelf above river gorge R with wooded hills rising L. Continue through fields and woods and fork L to pass through Rheinsfelden (accommodation, refreshments). Turn L by Eglisau-Glattfelden dam and bear R. At crossroads turn L under railway and continue through Glattfelden (refreshments). Next junction is complicated. Bear L on cycle track immediately after village, turn R under road then zigzag up and over main road. Turn R to run parallel with main road on cycle track. Continue for 3km and just before junction in Weiach turn R on gravel track between fields. Turn L before railway, then R under bridge and L parallel to railway on asphalt track. The church at Hohentengen in Germany is visible across valley R. Follow railway, reaching main road just past **Kaiserstuhl** station (39.5km; 368m) (accommodation, refreshments, station). ▶

Kaiserstuhl (pop. 450), an attractive small town listed by Swiss Heritage, sits on a hillside overlooking the Rhine. The only remaining part of its medieval walls, Obere Turm tower at the top of the hill, can be visited. A partly cobbled main street, lined with old houses, links this tower with the river.

Kaiserstuhl and its larger German sister Hohentengen are linked by bridge. This is where the direct route from Schaffhausen rejoins.

Turn L over level crossing, bear R and immediately L on cycle track passing under roundabout. Continue ahead and after 50m turn R on quiet road between fields (Feldhofstrasse). Fork R at farm and drop down to emerge beside main road and pass under railway. Continue steadily downhill on asphalt cycle track beside road for 2km. After moving slightly away from road, turn R and L to continue following road. At bottom of hill, fork L following Dorfstrasse uphill through Rümikon (accommodation, refreshments). Fork R (Dorfstrasse) to continue following main road beyond village (no cycle lane). Turn L at next junction, pass under railway and turn immediately R parallel with railway. Continue past Mellikon, following Alte Landstrasse parallel to railway as far as possible before joining road on L. Continue past dam R, derelict factory L and station R into **Reckingen** (48.5km) (refreshments).

In middle of village turn R, then after 100m L and immediately R (Alte Dorfstrasse). Bear L and continue on asphalt cycle track parallel to railway. Pass large factory R, with hills rising immediately L. Continue

The thermal spa at Bad Zurzach

on quiet residential road (Breitestrasse) and join main road (Promenadestrasse) into spa town of **Bad Zurzach** (51.5km; 340m) (accommodation, refreshments, camping, tourist office, station).

> **Bad Zurzach** (pop. 4000) is home to Switzerland's largest thermal spa, with four outdoor pools and a wide range of other aquatic attractions. This is part of a large complex that includes a wellness centre, clinic and three hotels. The town's other attractions include the church of St Verena, a blend of Romanesque, Gothic and baroque styles.

Turn L (Hauptstrasse) and after 100m R (Quellestrasse) leading through gardens to thermal spa complex. Turn R (Dr.-Martin-Erb-Strasse) past main entrance to baths L. Turn L (Badstrasse), continuing past wellness centre and clinics to climb gently out of town through residential area. Drop down, crossing side road, and continue on Steigstrasse passing Rietheim R (refreshments, station). Fork R on asphalt cycle track to follow road and railway through narrow gap where hills come down close to Rhine. Continue on Tüftelstrasse, descending into **Koblenz** (57.5km) (station).

Continue on Achenbergerstrasse past Koblenz Dorf station, bearing R under railway to T-junction. Turn L (Landstrasse) and continue bearing L onto riverbank. Pass under railway bridge and turn R over Rhine through Swiss–German border post. ▶

Once over border ignore official cycle route signs (which use a very complicated system of cycle paths to negotiate the road junction ahead). Instead turn immediately L between industrial units, then after 100m R (Klingnauer Strasse) and L (Koblenzer Strasse). Cross road and continue into Jahnweg, passing campsite L and emerging on riverbank. Pass allotments R and swing away from river to pass behind swimming pool complex. Fork L on gravel track returning to riverbank with steep wooded cliffs R and Waldshut visible on hill ahead. Opposite boat landing stage turn R on track

R2 continues on Swiss side of river to Stein, opposite Bad Säckingen. Once over river, German D8 signs are followed to Bad Säckingen.

Kaiserstrasse, Waldshut, with the Rathaus on the left

To bypass Waldshut, follow D8 signs continuing along riverbank to rejoin route beyond town.

uphill (Zollstrasse), then L at top over bridge into centre of **Waldshut** (60km; 341m) (accommodation, refreshments, camping, tourist office, station). ◄

> **Waldshut** (pop. 23,000) stands on a bluff above the Rhine. Its principal attraction is Kaiserstrasse, a medieval pedestrianised main street running between 13th-century Schaffhauser Tor (the town gaol until 1864) and Basler Tor at the opposite end. The town brook flows through a gully down the middle of the street, which has three fountains and is lined with highly decorated buildings. The town is a very popular tourist destination.

STAGE 8
Waldshut to Basel

Start	Waldshut town hall (341m)
Finish	Basel Cathedral (254m)
Distance	68km
Signposting	D8 Waldshut–Bad Säckingen; R2 Stein–Basel

For this stage the route follows the north (German) bank of the Rhine, through a number of attractive medieval towns, before crossing to the Swiss side at Bad Säckingen. The landscape is fairly industrial between towns, increasingly so approaching Basel. Wooded hills still line both sides of valley, sometimes coming close to the river.

Leave **Waldshut** by Kaiserstrasse, pass through archway and bear L. Pass hospital L and bear L on cycle track beside main road. Drop down and continue along river-bank beside Baseler Strasse. Pass entrance to power station (*kraftwerk*) and take next L (Auweg). This curves L to river, then bears R through industrial estate. Shortly before road turns sharply R, fork L and immediately R on asphalt track between fields with allotments L. ▶ Turn L over canal and bear R on gravel track circling reservoir. Continue through trees on long island between Rhine R and canal L. At crossing of tracks, turn sharply R (asphalt) and cross canal. Head upstream R, then fork R and bear L under main road. Continue on cycle track to crossroads and head diagonally across. Follow road bearing L, and at T-junction turn R (Alte Landstrasse). Continue, bearing L on dual-use track, between road and railway for 2km through **Albbruck** (8.5km) (where road becomes Hauensteiner Strasse) and Albert to reach river again at Hauenstein (refreshments).

Cross main road and continue on Hauensteiner Strasse cut into cliff side following river, cycling on road with no cycle lane. Continue on Luttinger Strasse through Luttingen (accommodation, refreshments).

The domed building across Rhine L is Leibstadt, one of Switzerland's four nuclear power stations.

Bear L opposite church into Stadenhauser Strasse. This village street leads onto a country lane between fields. Fork R beside cemetery (Dr.-Rudolf-Eberle-Strasse), continuing through fields. Fork L before buildings to emerge on road. Cross road by staggered junction R/L into Rheinuferweg and continue under new Rhine road bridge to riverbank. Turn R on brick-block track over sidestream and follow riverbank with view of Laufenburg ahead. Pass swimming pool and playground, bearing R to reach road. Turn L (Andelsbachstrasse), climbing steeply, then bear L (Hauptstrasse), passing under archway into medieval **Laufenburg** (15.5km) (accommodation, refreshments, tourist office, station).

Laufenburg in Germany (pop. 4300) and Laufenburg in Switzerland (pop. 3200) stand on opposite sides of the Rhine. They were once one community until divided by Napoleon's redrawing of European borders in 1801. Both towns have attractive medieval centres with colourful riverside houses, made quieter by the removal of through traffic when a new bridge opened upstream in 2004.

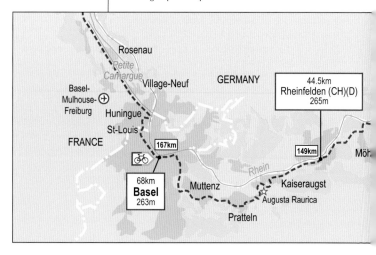

Continue down cobbled main street, passing bridge at bottom L, and climb to cross railway by L level crossing. Bear L, passing station L, and follow asphalt lane climbing through woods and over ridge. Continue along residential street (Zimmermannstrasse) and turn L onto dual-use path L of main road. Turn L after 400m, over level crossing (Kraftwerkweg) and R along asphalt track following river. Just after swimming pool L, turn L between baths and car park. Drop down to river and turn R over sidestream, passing **Murg** (19km) (accommodation, refreshments, tourist office, cycle shop, station).

Continue on asphalt track beside river (Rheinuferweg), zigzagging R and L after sewerage works. Follow railway for 4km, with Rhine and later allotments L, until just after dam and power station L. Bear L into Rheinallee and continue parallel to river with view of Bad Säckingen covered bridge ahead. Pass defensive tower L and turn second R into cobbled Fischergasse. Turn L (Steinbrückstrasse) into centre of **Bad Säckingen** (25.5km; 291m) (accommodation, refreshments, tourist office, cycle shop, station).

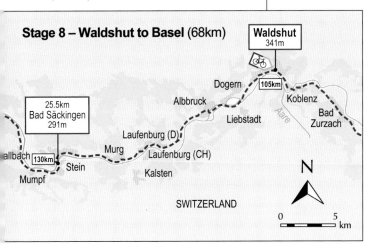

Stage 8 – Waldshut to Basel (68km)

101

Bad Säckingen has the longest covered bridge over the Rhine

The Trumpeter of Säckingen

This turn is easily missed. If you miss it, continue on main road for 250m and turn R at next turn (Steinackerstrasse).

In addition to having a heavily baroqued Gothic cathedral (St Fridolin) and Europe's longest covered bridge, **Bad Säckingen** (pop. 17,000) is best known as the setting for a romantic epic poem, *The Trumpeter of Säckingen*, written in 1853 by Joseph von Scheffel. This tells the story of Werner (a lowly trumpeter) and titled Margareta, for whom social difference made marriage impossible. The story is narrated by a cat (Kater Hiddigeigei) that observes all that happens in the town.

Cross Münsterplatz with St Fridolin's church L, leaving square R with police station L. After 50m turn L (Rheinbrückstrasse) and continue over Rhine into Switzerland on Holzbrücke, the most attractive of all the covered wooden bridges over the river. Bear R, climbing to reach main road. Turn R (Schaffhauserstrasse) and continue through **Stein** (26.5km). At end of village, where R2 rejoins, follow main road bearing R with Rhine below R. Pass campsite R and continue through **Mumpf** (29km) (accommodation, refreshments, station).

At end of village, fork R through barriers (Rheinweg). ◀ Continue following river on Rheinstrasse.

Fork R to follow Rheinstrasse through **Wallbach** (31km) (accommodation, refreshments, cycle shop).

Continue out of village, climbing a little away from river past small industrial estate and into forest. ▶ Once in forest bear R, winding through trees and at junction turn R (Wererhyweg) and continue alongside river. Pass picnic place and continue into Haümattlirhyweg. At T-junction turn R (Cholhüttweg) and R again (Cholhütterhyweg). Fork R (Chrabisrhyweg) and pass Chrabis fishing club R. Continue onto Burkliweg out of forest with field L.

After first field turn L onto asphalt road between fields. Pass factory L, bearing R to T-junction. Turn L, passing swimming pool complex R. At T-junction turn R uphill and just before road, R again on cycle track along front of baths (39km). Bear L under road, then follow track as it circles car park R and passes back under road on Swimmbadstrasse. Turn L, crossing stream and climbing steeply past campsite R. At top bear R onto gravel track and bear L alongside forest on Waldrandstrasse. Cross asphalt road and at second junction bear L to follow Waldrandstrasse away from forest, past farm R and two towers topped with stork nests L that were originally shafts for salt mines. Cross road towards factory, and just before its gate turn R alongside factory and sharp L to pass behind it. At T-junction turn R into forest, parallel with railway. This track comes out above Rhine downstream of Rheinfelden dam and power station R. Continue on gravel track, bearing R behind houses L and turn L by Zähringer Taverne into Roberstenstrasse, a quiet residential street with thermal baths R. Turn R at T-junction, and bear L under Storchenturm (Storks Tower) into **Rheinfelden** (44.5km; 265m) (accommodation, refreshments, tourist office, cycle shop, station).

Continue through old centre of Rheinfelden on cobbled Kupfergasse, which becomes Marktgasse, passing baroque town hall with murals R. Pass end of Rheinbrücke R (the oldest Rhine bridge below Konstanz) and continue along Habich-Dietschy-Strasse. Bear R on cycle track to T-junction and turn R, passing old Feldschlossen brewery steam engine on roundabout (brewery is visible behind

For 6km path is in forest, following network of gravel *waldstrassen* (forest tracks). Route is well signposted R2. Unless otherwise shown, rule is always bear R following river.

Old salt mine shafts with stork nests near Möhlin

houses L). Continue on cycle track beside main road for 4.5km, passing behind a pond, crossing two motorway bridges and a railway bridge, and passing an industrial area R. At beginning of **Kaiseraugst** (accommodation, refreshments), where cycle track drops down R, turn L into Giebenacherstrasse, passing through housing estates. Take third turn R (Schwarzackerstrasse, becoming Venusstrasse) and after 500m R into (another) Giebernacherstrasse. This runs downhill through ruins of **Augusta Raurica** (51.5km), with Roman amphitheatre L and museum R.

Augusta Raurica was one of three Roman colonial cities established by Emperor Augustus as part of his campaign to conquer the central Alps around 15BC (the others were modern-day Augsburg and Aosta). At its peak in the second century AD, it housed 20,000 citizens and had all the amenities of an important Roman city, including forum, amphitheatre and aqueduct, several temples and public baths, and the largest Roman theatre north of the Alps,

with 10,000 seats. Severely damaged by an earth-
quake in AD250 and attacked by the Alemanni tribe
soon after, it was abandoned in favour of a smaller,
heavily fortified site on the banks of the Rhine.

Turn L (Schulstrasse) beside school L, zigzag R and
L past new houses and fork R on asphalt cycle track.
Drop down to cross stream on covered bridge and turn
L at T-junction. Turn L at crosspaths, continuing with
stream L past allotments R and under motorway. Ignore
turning immediately after bridge and take next R over
motorway. At T-junction turn R (Im Wannenboden) past
distribution depot and L at next junction. Cross roundabout into Mühleweg and continue over level crossing
along residential street. Join Oberemattstrasse and turn L
(Hauptstrasse). Follow this round bend R and fork R past
fountain to reach centre of **Pratteln** (55.5km) (accommodation, refreshments, cycle shop, station).

Continue into Schmiedestrasse, bearing L and R to
follow Mayenfelserstrasse, becoming Wartenbergstrasse,
for 1km. At T-junction turn R and ahead over crossroads
(Kasteliweg). Turn L on cycle track parallel with tram-
lines R (Baslerstrasse) and factories behind. Continue

*Basel Cathedral and
cable ferry*

past tram turning circle and follow Breitstrasse as it bears L. At T-junction turn R downhill (Burggasse). Straight over at crossroads into Kirchplatz, with church R, into centre of **Muttenz** (60km) (accommodation, refreshments, cycle shop).

Turn L uphill (Geispelgasse), and after 40m turn R (Pfaffenmattweg). Continue onto Froscheneckweg between allotments R and wooded hillside L. Turn R and L at offset crossroads and continue with allotments R and wooded hillside L. Bear L through woods, turn R over motorway bridge and continue over stream on covered bridge. Turn R past flats L, passing under road bridge into parkland. Pass dinosaur statue L and continue through middle of park with wide range of sporting facilities. At park exit cross tram tracks, turning R on cycle track with **St Jakob Park** (Basel FC ground) ahead. Turn first L into Birsstrasse, passing under railway and motorway bridges, continuing through residential area. Bear R parallel to railway bridge, cross main road and

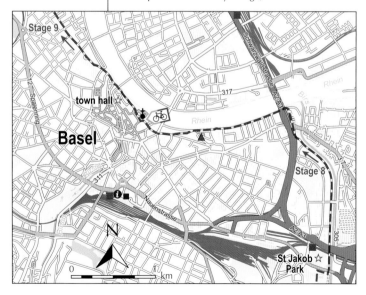

continue with railway above to Rhine bank. Turn L along quayside (St Alban-Rheinweg) with Basel Cathedral visible ahead. ▶ 400m before Rhine bridge, fork L steeply uphill (Mühlenberg) and continue on St Alban-Vorstadt. Cross main road into Rittergasse, with elegant houses, and bear L into Münsterplatz in front of **Basel Cathedral** (68km; 254m) (accommodation, refreshments, YH, tourist office, cycle shop, station).

To reach YH turn L (signposted) 100m before reaching Mühlenberg.

The urban area of **Basel** extends from Switzerland into France and Germany, giving it the title of Drei Landes Stadt (three-country city). It owes its importance to its position at the head of the navigable Rhine, and is Switzerland's only port. Built in 1225, Basel Bridge was for many years the only bridge over the Rhine between Rotterdam and Konstanz. For over 500 years from AD999, the city was ruled by Prince-Bishops from their powerbase around Basel Münster (cathedral), built between 1019 and 1500 on a hill overlooking a river bend. In 1521, local trade guilds asserted their supremacy and power moved to the Rathaus (town hall) and guild houses below the hill.

Among the most photographed sights are four cable-operated pedestrian ferries that are propelled across the river by force of the current and use no external power. Modern-day Basel is dominated by chemical and pharmaceutical industries. Novartis, formed by merger of two Basel-based pharmaceutical giants, Ciba-Geigy and Sandoz, is redeveloping its factory and laboratories into an integrated development campus, with stunning new buildings by contemporary architects including Frank Geary. This has required rerouting the cycle track north out of the city around Novartis campus.

STAGE 9
Basel to Neuf-Brisach

Start	Basel Cathedral (263m)
Finish	Place d'Armes, Neuf-Brisach (194m)
Distance	66km
Signposting	RR with deviations (from French border)

In this stage, the Rhine turns north, forming the border between France and Germany. The route enters France through a wide, flat, agricultural valley, with large areas of forest. Once clear of Basel this stage leaves the river to follow canal towpaths, forest trails and a dismantled railway through southern Alsace.

Hüningerstrasse originally continued through Novartis campus directly to Huningue in France. In 2009 a land swap led to this road being closed and the route was diverted around the outside of Novartis through a new Swiss–French border post.

From **Basel Cathedral** head N, leaving cobbled Münsterplatz by Augustinergasse, continuing past a fountain R into Rheinsprung, overlooking river and Mittlere Rheinbrücke. Drop steeply down, crossing tram tracks into Schifflände. Continue N past Les Trois Rois hotel R into Blumenrain, forking L beside Predigerkirche church into Spitalstrasse. Continue past hospital L, and ahead at offset crossroads into Lothringerstrasse, a quiet residential street. At roundabout take second exit (Hüningerstrasse). ◄

Turn L into main road (Elsässerstrasse) with Novartis campus R. Fork R before tram turning circle and turn sharply R (Kohlenstrasse). Bear L (straight on leads into Novartis), across roundabout and through Swiss–French border post. Bear L on cycle track beside new road (D107) following this past car parks and sports fields. Bear L (Rue de l'Industrie) and keep L to pass behind another large car park before returning to road. Bear L, then turn R at roundabout (Rue de la Chapelle) and ahead at offset crossroads into Rue des 3 Frontières to reach Rhine. Turn L (Quai du Rhin), alongside river, and where road bears L, fork R on track following river. Just

before sluice gates, turn L and immediately R under road to emerge on asphalt towpath at start of Canal du Rhône au Rhin in **Huningue** (5km) (accommodation, refreshments, camping, tourist office).

Parc des Eaux Vives in an old canal basin at Huningue

For the next 25km route follows canal towpath. Immediately after Huningue sluice, pass watersports park R with white-water canoe slalom course. ▶ Pass **Village-Neuf** (7.5km) (refreshments) and enter **Petite Camargue** wildlife reserve (10km) with bird-watching hides L. At Haberhaeuser, where there is an interpretation centre for the reserve, cross canal to R bank by two bridges via lock island. Cross back to L bank at **Rosenau** (12km), returning to R bank at **Kembs** (18km; 241m) (refreshments).

Alongside the gravel towpath there are representations of the planets, showing their size and relative distances from the sun.

Pass behind marina and after 1km bear away from canal, passing under two road bridges and crossing lock on branch canal to reach **Le Corbusier sluice** (21km). Just before sluice gates, turn sharply L over canal on new bridge and turn R on far bank to resume following now wider canal on asphalt towpath. Pass under road bridge and continue past small mound with viewpoint L, to reach road bridge at **Pont du Bouc** (30km).

Old lifting bridge over the canal at Kembs

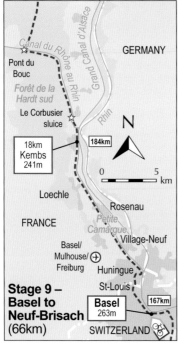

**Stage 9 –
Basel to
Neuf-Brisach
(66km)**

At the end of November 1944, a now almost forgotten battle took place at **Pont du Bouc** when Allied (mostly French colonial) troops withstood a fierce counter-attack by the retreating German army. In six days of fighting, 1500 French troops were killed, more than these same units had lost during five months of fighting in Italy. After many years of lobbying, a memorial was inaugurated in May 2011.

Pass under bridge, then turn L up and over bridge on cycle track beside road. Bear L onto slip road and turn R on cycle track into forest. For the next 14km follow this track through the **Forêt Domaniale de la Hardt nord**. Pass memorial to a dead soldier L, cross motorway and bear R alongside railway. Cross level crossing L and busy road, forking R ahead at **Grunhutte** (34.5km) to continue through forest. Cross three local roads, after third of which track becomes quiet road. Pass equestrian centre, and turn R at next road (D50) out of forest into **Blodelsheim** (47.5km; 210m) (accommodation, refreshments).

Turn L at roundabout (D468), passing through village and continuing on cycle track beside road to **Fessenheim** (50.5km) (accommodation, refreshments).

400m after end of cycle track, and before main part of Fessenheim is reached, turn L (Rue des Tilleuls). ▶ After 700m, turn R onto obvious cycle track along route of dismantled railway. Follow this for 4km, passing through Fessenheim and **Balgau** (53.5km), ignoring RR signs taking you into Balgau. At junction with D468 bear L along cycle track beside road and after 250m turn sharply R (sp Restaurant Pélerin, Thierhurst). At T-junction, turn L, passing **Thierhurst** R (56km) (refreshments).

This turn is easily missed as RR sign is hidden by honeysuckle.

A restaurant, barn and church are all that remain of the medieval village of **Thierhurst**, which disappeared in the 14th century, probably as a result of flooding but possibly due to destruction by German invaders. Pilgrims visit the church to view a wooden pietà (representation of the Virgin Mary holding the dead Christ), carved from a fire-damaged tree trunk and alleged to have miraculous powers.

Continue to **Heiteren** (58.5km), turning R (Rue du Rhin) and soon after leaving village turn L to follow cycle track along dismantled railway for another 4.5km, passing **Obersaasheim** (61km) (accommodation, refreshments, camping). Where track reaches edge of **Algolsheim** (63.5km) (accommodation), turn L

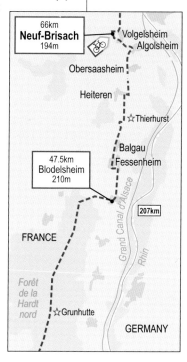

111

The carved pietà at Thierhurst is said to have miraculous powers

on cycle track beside road (Route de Neuf-Brisach). Pass under main road into Rue du Poilu and ahead at first roundabout past extensive barracks R. After water tower L, turn R at next roundabout (Voie Romaine) and L at final roundabout (another Rue de Neuf-Brisach) past sawmills R and over canal. Turn R (Rue de Bâle), crossing series of moats and fortifications, and continue through Porte de Bâle to reach central square (Place d'Armes) of fortified **Neuf-Brisach** (66km; 194m) (accommodation, refreshments, camping, tourist office, cycle shop).

Neuf-Brisach (pop. 2200) is a well-preserved example of an early 18th-century model fortified town. After France lost the important riverside town of Breisach (east of the Rhine) to the Habsburgs in 1697, the celebrated military engineer Vauban was commissioned to design a new fortified town to guard the border. Neuf-Brisach was Vauban's final work and one of his greatest. The town is enclosed by an octagonal bastion wall with guardhouses and

four gateways, surrounded by a system of concentric star-shaped earthworks that take up a larger area than the town itself. Within the walls, a grid street system had separate areas allocated to public buildings, private residences and military installations, all grouped around a large central square.

Fortifications at Neuf-Brisach, designed by Vauban

STAGE 10
Neuf-Brisach to Strasbourg

Start	Place d'Armes, Neuf-Brisach (194m)
Finish	Quai Louis Pasteur, Strasbourg (140m)
Distance	69km
Signposting	RR with deviations

Continuing through rural France, this stage follows a canal towpath right to the heart of Strasbourg, through a wide, flat, agricultural valley dotted with villages. There are views of the Vosges mountains (west) and the Black Forest (east), although this is the only stage where the Rhine is never seen. This region has been heavily fought over and there are numerous remnants of past conflicts.

Leave **Neuf-Brisach** by Rue de Strasbourg, passing through Porte de Strasbourg and turning immediately R on cycle track parallel with railway L. Cross canal and turn L at main road over level crossing. At roundabout, cross first exit and bear ahead R on cycle track (sp RR Biesheim), continuing through fields to **Biesheim** (4km) (accommodation, refreshments, camping, tourist office).

At roundabout turn R (Rue du Giessen), ahead over series of crossing roads and turn L at T-junction (Rue des Pêcheurs). Keep ahead at traffic lights (Place de l'École) and bear R beyond school R (Rue des Bergers). Take second exit at roundabout, passing through car park to follow cycle track winding through fields. Pass cemetery L and bear R to cross small canal. Turn L on cycle track beside main road and bear L onto towpath of larger canal R. Follow this for 3km to beginning of **Kunheim** (9km).

Do not enter village. Bear R on gravel continuation of towpath dropping under main road, parallel to canal. Bear R to join towpath alongside **Canal du Rhône au Rhin**, and after 600m bear L to cross canal and continue following towpath. After 4km, bear L alongside

Cycle route along the towpath of the Canal du Rhône au Rhin

branch canal from Colmar, pass under first bridge and turn sharply back L to cross canal. Bear R and L to rejoin Canal du Rhône au Rhin and follow this along recently restored towpath for 60km. ▸

Canal passes close to **Artzenheim** (14.5km) (accommodation, refreshments), **Marckolsheim** (19.5km; 176m) (accommodation, refreshments, camping, tourist office, cycle shop), where Ligne Maginot Museum is worth visiting, and **Sundhouse** (30.5km) (accommodation, refreshments), before joining wider, navigable canal at **Neunkirch** (39km).

Marckolsheim is the site of a museum dedicated to the **Maginot Line**, the world's second greatest defensive structure after the Great Wall of China. Built between 1930 and 1940 to hold back attacks on France from the east, it consisted of a series of fortifications, including concrete bunkers, gun posts and tank traps. Along the north-east sector, the line was continuous, with its own electricity generation, telephone and underground railway systems. The southern sectors, including that around Marckolsheim, were less heavily fortified, as the Rhine was seen

The towpath alongside the disused Rhône–Rhine canal has been restored as part of a through cycle route from Colmar to Strasbourg.

Stage 10 – Neuf Brisach to Strasbourg (69km)

Sundhouse

FRANCE

Canal du Rhône au Rhin

Rhin

19.5km
Marckolsheim
176m

☆ Ligne Maginot Museum

N

Artzenheim

0 — 5 km

Kunheim

GERMANY

Neuf-Brisach
194m

Biesheim

226km Breisach
am Rhein

🚴 Volgelsheim

Algolsheim

as the principal barrier to invasion. The line was effective in preventing an attack from the east; however, when invasion came in 1940, the German army simply bypassed these defences, sweeping through Belgium to attack France from the north.

Cross canal at Neunkirch lock for short section on R bank, recrossing to L bank at **Boofzheim** lock (41.5km). Continue along towpath lined with mature trees, crossing a wide river (branch of River Ill) at **Krafft** (51.5km) (accommodation, refreshments).

Continue past **Eschau** (58.5km) (accommodation, refreshments), and into Strasbourg suburbs at **Illkirch-Graffenstaden** (63km) (accommodation, refreshments, cycle shop), after which route leaves towpath temporarily to follow Rue des Lilas parallel with canal. Before yellow overbridge, where road turns away L, continue on

Petite-France, Strasbourg

cycle track ahead for 40m then turn L immediately beside bridge. Turn R, passing under a road bridge and follow road (on cycle track R) bearing R to cross canal at lock. In middle of bridge turn R, dropping down to canal, and sharply L back onto cycle track, now on R bank of canal. Continue N, between canal and Rue du Doubs, passing large industrial estate R and Strasbourg prison beyond motorway A35 L. Pass lock and continue under railway and road bridges. Bear L following canal past Strasbourg rowing club and mosque. After railway bridge bear L, taking lower route under next road bridge. Turn back sharply R after bridge, climbing to cross river on cycle bridge beside road. This brings you to Quai Louis Pasteur, from where it is a short distance to centre of **Strasbourg** (69km; 140m) (accommodation, refreshments, YH, camping, tourist office, cycle shop, station). ▶

To reach centre of Strasbourg, continue straight ahead away from canal (Rue Humann), following cycle signs for Centre Ville.

Strasbourg Cathedral, floodlit at night

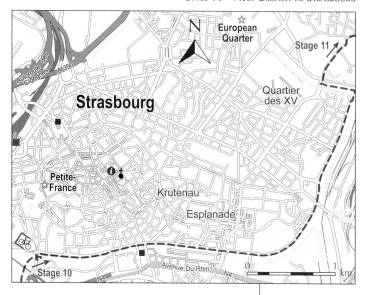

Fought over for centuries and governed alternatively by France (1681–1870, 1919–40 and since
1945) and Germany (1871–1918, 1940–44),
Strasbourg (pop. in metropolitan area 640,000)
nowadays sees itself as an international city, home
to many transnational European institutions (see
Stage 11). The city centre is concentrated around
the medieval streets of Grande Île, an island in L'Ill
river (a tributary of the Rhine), which is dominated
by the Gothic sandstone cathedral (completed in
1439) – its spire made the cathedral the world's tallest building when it was built. The most attractive
area of the city is Petite-France, with its network of
narrow canals bordered by numerous half-timbered
houses. Nearby are Barrage Vauban and Ponts
Couverts with its four bridge towers. Strasbourg port
is the second largest on the Rhine (after Duisburg).

STAGE 11
Strasbourg to Drusenheim

Start	Quai Louis Pasteur, Strasbourg (140m)
Finish	Drusenheim ferry (124m)
Distance	33km
Signposting	RR, with deviations

Continuing through France, this short stage passes through residential suburbs of Strasbourg before closely following the Rhine. The route is mostly through woods, running on or beside the river flood dyke.

Leave **Strasbourg** along N side of main canal running east to west, S of city centre. This starts as Quai Louis Pasteur, with hospital L and canal R. Continue ahead on cycle track R of road as name changes to Quai Fustel de Coulanges, then Quai du Général Koenig and finally Quai des Alpes. The approaches to five bridges are crossed. ◀ Follow quayside as it bears L along Quai des Belges under another bridge and continues, firstly as Rue Général Picquart becoming Rue du Général Conrad. Where this turns away from canal, bear R to follow cycle track along canal side and continue round bend L at canal junction. At approach to first bridge, bear L climbing up to bridge and turn R over canal. ◀

Major work has been undertaken to revive the dock area on the opposite side of the canal.

To visit Strasbourg's European Quarter, do not cross canal, rather continue ahead for 1km to reach main European buildings on both sides of canal.

Its transnational position on the borders of France and Germany has made Strasbourg an attractive location for many important European government and legal institutions. High-tech buildings, housing many of these, can be found in the **European Quarter** (Quartier Européen) at the intersection of the Marne–Rhine canal and the River L'Ill, northeast of the city centre. These include the Medicines Directorate, Court of Human Rights and Agora

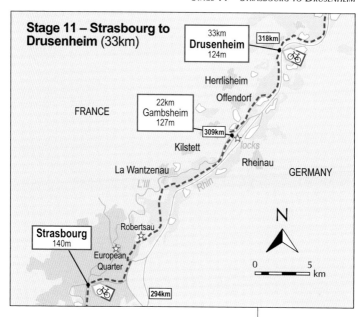

Stage 11 – Strasbourg to Drusenheim (33km)

33km
Drusenheim
124m
318km

Herrlisheim

Offendorf

FRANCE

22km
Gambsheim
127m
309km

Kilstett

La Wantzenau

L'Ill

Rhin

Rheinau

GERMANY

locks

Strasbourg
140m

Robertsau

European Quarter

294km

N

0   5
km

*Petite-France,
Strasbourg*

The European Parliament at Strasbourg

Château de Pourtalès at Robertsau, now a hotel

office building (north of the canal), the Council of Europe and European Ombudsman (south of the canal) and the European Parliament (in the fork between the canal and L'Ill). The location in Strasbourg of the latter has caused considerable controversy, as there are also Parliament buildings in Brussels and Luxembourg, causing parliamentary members, officers and staff to live peripatetic lives between these three cities.

Continue ahead (Chemin Goeb) on cycle track R as road winds through residential area becoming Rue de la Carpe Haute then bear L (Chemin du Beulenwoerth). Cycle track crosses to L where road becomes Rue de la Lamproie, then ends at roundabout. Turn R (Rue Mélanie) and follow this to entrance of Château de Pourtalès at **Robertsau** (7.5km).

Bear R, following cycle route signs around car park, and turn L through barrier into parkland. Cycle track runs ahead on top of flood dyke for 6.5km winding through forested parkland. Cross small bridge over stream feeding lagoon R and fork R (sp la Wantzenau) beside moat of long-vanished fort and continue on dyke through farmland. At next path junction ignore RR signs L, instead keep ahead and continue following flood dyke into woodland of Bois Communal de la Wantzenau (13.5km). ▶

To reach la Wantzenau (1.5km) (accommodation, refreshments, cycle shop, station), fork L and follow signposts.

Continue past small bird sanctuary and zoo R and after 1km turn R off dyke. Continue to Rhine bank and turn L along road running below main flood dyke. This is a quiet road, which is closed to private vehicles and used to test cars from General Motors car factory in Strasbourg. At a barrier after 1km, turn R and L along

2000-year-old fossilised log found in a gravel pit at Offendorf

When car testing is not taking place, the barrier is open and cyclists can continue on road below flood dyke to Gambsheim dam.

gravel track on top of flood dyke. ◄ Follow this for 6km, to reach **Gambsheim locks** and dam (22km; 127m) (refreshments).

Turn L away from dam, cross drainage canal and turn sharply L at roundabout (sp Offendorf). Continue through middle of aggregates works, and 500m beyond these turn R to reach river. Turn L, making your way around piles of gravel awaiting shipment. Loose gravel surface at first, which soon becomes compacted. After 600m, bear L away from river on flood dyke between fields L and woods R, forking R to continue on dyke where it turns into woods. Continue ahead on asphalt road alongside dyke for 5km to reach **Drusenheim ferry** (33km; 124m) (refreshments). ◄

To reach Drusenheim (1.5km) (accommodation, refreshments, cycle shop, station), turn L and follow Rue du Rhin into village.

Drusenheim (pop. 5100) was liberated by US troops on 12 December 1944, with little damage. However, a German counter-offensive, which recaptured the town on 5 January 1945, and a subsequent American assault on 20 January, destroyed 85% of buildings and caused many civilian casualties.

STAGE 12
Drusenheim to Karlsruhe

Start	Drusenheim ferry (124m)
Finish	Karlsruhe station (115m)
Distance	56km
Signposting	RR (in France only)

This stage closely follows the Rhine through the north-west corner of French Alsace, mostly along flood dykes through riverside woodlands and past a number of sand and gravel pits. Towards the end, Germany is reached and the river crossed en route to Karlsruhe, where a network of cycle tracks through parkland enables you to bypass industrial areas along the riverbank and reach the city centre without venturing onto any roads.

From **Drusenheim ferry**, continue N on French side of river on cycle track along top of flood dyke. This is followed for 25km to Seltz, with a few diversions around aggregate works and lagoons. At first junction take middle track (ahead L) following flood dyke round aggregates quay. Return to river and continue for some distance passing two more aggregates quays. Dog-leg L and R to cross Moder river (an old Rhine course) and continue alongside Moder, passing under road serving **Iffezheim dam** and locks (16.5km).

Continue ahead, passing point where Moder joins Rhine. After 1km, turn L away from river for short distance and R to regain flood dyke. Pass round marina R and bear R to continue under Wintersdorf combined road and rail bridge. 350m beyond bridge, bear L, then L again up onto flood dyke and R passing round **Beinheim** port (20km) with industrial area L. At end of port turn L and then R on flood dyke running between fields L and trees R, passing Alsace's largest heronry with around 160 breeding pairs of herons. ▶ Follow this as it turns to run parallel to river (200m R). Pass waterworks L, then fork R to riverbank to reach **Seltz ferry** (25km) (refreshments, camping).

Going straight ahead at R turn after Beinheim port will bring you to Beinheim (1.5km) (accommodation, refreshments, camping).

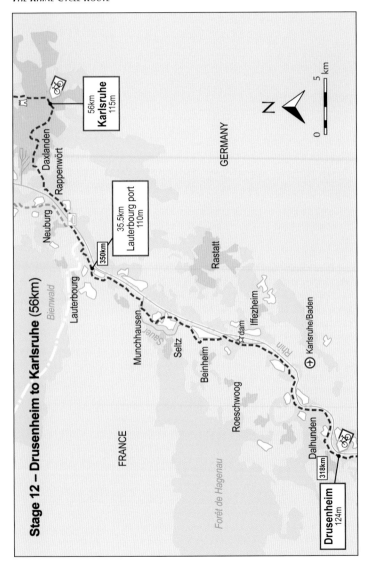

Stage 12 – Drusenheim to Karlsruhe (56km)

Continue across ferry ramp to join road along river-bank passing campsite and car parks L. This is a popular place on hot days as bathing beach has been created in lagoon L. Bear L away from river through aggregates works and L again to curve around another lagoon and enter Delta de la Sauer Nature Reserve. Follow cycle track winding in and out of trees with water meadows L and cross **Munchhausen** Bridge over River Sauer (29km) (accommodation, refreshments, camping).

Reed collectors' punts on River Sauer, Munchhausen

> **Munchhausen** occupies a tranquil location overlooking the River Sauer, a backwater that, before 19th-century navigational improvements, was the main course of the Rhine. Traditional punts, once used for fishing but now mainly for harvesting reeds, line the banks, and water fowl are numerous.

Turn R onto flood dyke and follow this round mouth of River Sauer. Cross road and continue along dyke with flood ditch R to reach fork where asphalt track bears L then turns sharply L to circle a lagoon, passing through aggregates plant. Turn R at T-junction and bear L on road crossing railway. Turn R at next T-junction. ▶ Follow road over railway again down to riverbank beside restaurant at **Lauterbourg port** (35.5km; 110m) (refreshments).

If you turn L at T-junction you reach Lauterbourg (1.5km) (accommodation, refreshments, camping, tourist office, cycle shop, station).

Lauterbourg, the most easterly town in France

Lauterbourg (pop. 2200) is a French border town surrounded on three sides by German territory, and is the easternmost town in mainland France. Attractions include the parish church above square, attractive townhouses, ruined fortifications and gatehouses.

The bridge over the tiny River Lauter is the French–German border

Turn L along riverbank for 1km and bear L up onto flood dyke. Cross French–German border at small bridge over Alte Lauter river and continue on asphalt track to **Neuburg ferry** (41.5km) (refreshments on E bank).

The Neuburg ferry is used to cross the Rhine to reach Karlsruhe

Cross Rhine by ferry and follow road zigzagging away from river. Ignore first sharp turn L into forest (sp cycle route Karlsruhe), turning L instead at next turn where road passes through flood dyke. Follow 4wd track initially beside dyke but soon climbing onto top and continue for 3km to reach **Rappenwört** swimming baths (45.5km).

Turn R immediately before baths and follow road bearing L round baths to reach tram turning circle. Turn R and R again, following road towards Karlsruhe with car park L and tramway R. Continue on cycle lane beside road, crossing tramway after first station onto dedicated cycle track alongside sports fields. Fork L in middle of next turning circle, cross main road and continue along Willi-Egler-Strasse, a residential street parallel with main road L. On bend R, leave road onto cycle track L winding through grassy recreational area. Cross side road, main road and tramway in quick succession. Cross stream and immediately turn sharply R, dropping down to follow stream away from road. This stream, the Alb, is crossed five more times following a cycle track through parkland for 6km (sp Karlsruhe Bahnhof).

Cycle alongside stream, crossing it at second bridge. Cross back at next bridge, turning immediately R, with allotments L and weir R, and continue under two road bridges. Cross stream again on red and orange bridge, turning L along other bank. Fork L, dropping down concrete ramp under a series of bridges (there is a motorway junction high above) and continue following cycle track alongside stream. Pass under road bridge and continue for some distance, with stream and recreational facilities L and motorway R. Pass under tramway bridge and cross stream again, turning R under three more motorway bridges (another junction). Continue under road bridge, cross stream again and pass cascade R. Climb up to crossroad, finally leaving stream, and continue on cycle track between trees with railway R. Continue

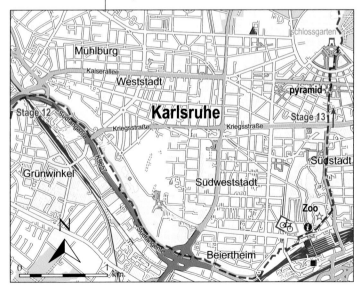

through allotments and cross tramway. Turn R to re-cross tramway just in front of tram terminus building. Cross Schwarzwaldstrasse and continue ahead (Victor-Gollancz-Strasse) to reach **Karlsruhe** station (56km; 115m) (accommodation, refreshments, YH, camping, tourist office, cycle shop, station).

Schloss Karlsruhe and statue of Margrave Karl Wilhelm II

> Founded in 1715 by Margrave Karl Wilhelm II, **Karlsruhe** (pop. 295,000) is a relatively modern city. At its centre is the Schloss Karlsruhe palace from which 32 streets radiate, giving the city its nickname Fachterstadt (fan city). It is said that Karlsruhe's layout provided inspiration for Washington DC. Marktplatz, south of the palace, is the commercial centre, with the Rathaus (town hall) and evangelical church. In the middle of Marktplatz is a pyramid, the city's emblem, covering Karl Wilhelm's tomb. Karlsruhe is home to Germany's two highest courts, the Federal Constitutional Court and the Court of Appeals. Germany's largest oil refinery can be found beside the Rhine, west of the city.

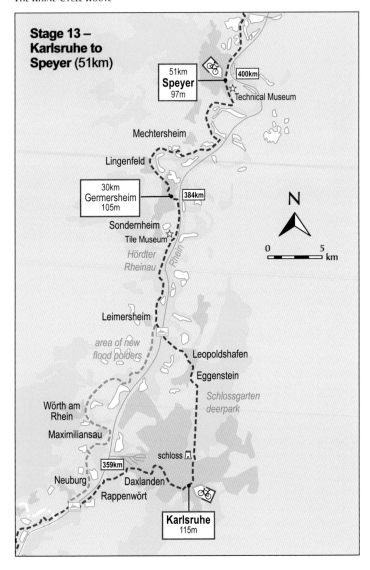

Stage 13 –
Karlsruhe to
Speyer (51km)

51km
Speyer
97m

400km

Technical Museum

Mechtersheim

Lingenfeld

30km
Germersheim
105m

384km

Sondernheim

Tile Museum

*Hördter
Rheinau*

Rhein

N

0   5
km

Leimersheim

*area of new
flood polders*

Leopoldshafen

Eggenstein

*Schlossgarten
deerpark*

Wörth am
Rhein

Maximiliansau

schloss

Neuburg

359km

Daxlanden

Rappenwört

Karlsruhe
115m

STAGE 13
Karlsruhe to Speyer

Start	Karlsruhe station (115m)
Finish	Klipfelsau, Speyer (97m)
Distance	51km
Signposting	RR (from Leimersheim)

The route leaves Karlsruhe on a straight track through the Schlossgarten deer park. Heading back to, and crossing, the Rhine, the path meanders through forest and fields, following flood dykes around long-since-abandoned bends in the river. The landscape is generally flat and mostly agricultural, with industry at Germersheim and approaching Speyer.

RR follows the west bank of the Rhine from Neuburg (Stage 11) to Speyer. Between Wörth am Rhein (opposite Karlsruhe) and Leimersheim major works are underway building new dykes around large holding lakes (polder) intended to absorb abnormal river flows and prevent a repeat of the catastrophic floods of 1995. This has led to path diversions, some of them permanent, which take the cycle route well away from the Rhine. This guide avoids affected areas by keeping to the east bank from Karlsruhe, returning to the west bank at Leimersheim.

From **Karlsruhe** station, head diagonally R across Bahnhofplatz, crossing tramway and passing entrance to **zoo** L, into Am Stadtgarten. Follow cycle lane on pavement L alongside zoo. At end turn L alongside Ettlinger Strasse, cross street at first crossing and continue N on cycle track alongside road. Pass state theatre R, continuing along Karl-Friedrich-Strasse into Marktplatz with **pyramid** in centre of square and town hall L. Continue N and enter gates of **Schloss Karlsruhe** palace (2.5km).

Head half R across forecourt to enter **Schlossgarten** by arch R of central building. Turn immediately R and follow path bearing L between lawns L and trees R. At end turn R and continue past lake L. Follow path to far end of lake and turn R through red sandstone gate into

Pyramid over Karl Wilhelm II's tomb in Marktplatz, Karlsruhe

deer park. Continue straight ahead through forest for 6km on dual-use cycle/pedestrian track, with slight dog-leg L to cross ring road by bridge. Cross main road and after 1km turn L at crossing of forest paths (sp Radweg Rheinfahre Leimersheim). Cross motorway bridge, continuing through market gardens into **Eggenstein** (10km).

Pass fire station L and turn R on cycle track parallel to tramway. Continue through residential areas until point where tramway bears L. Cross stream, turn L over tramway and continue to main road. Turn R alongside road, then cross over onto cycle track on opposite side and after 50m fork L downhill (Am Sandberg). Follow track into **Leopoldshafen** (12.5km) and fork L (Blumenstrasse). At staggered crossroads turn L (Wiesenstrasse) and after 50m R (Am Südhang). At end turn L and follow road bearing R to sports club. Pass club entrance R and immediately fork R on gravel track parallel with flood dyke L. After 2km turn L onto road and follow this to **Leimersheim ferry** (16km) (refreshments).

Cross Rhine and follow road away from river. After bend R, turn L on cycle track through woods, following this to reach flood dyke. Turn R and soon come to junction with road to **Leimersheim** (17.5km; 105m). ▶

Continue winding along beside flood dyke for 7km, at first with fields L and woods R, but later through woodland of **Hördter Rheinaue** Nature Reserve. Cross sluice gates of Altrhein and turn R after restaurant (refreshments). Continue beside flood dyke with views of Sondernheim L, then turn R on road dropping down to riverbank. Pass old tile works L, now housing industrial locomotive museum and **tile museum** (26km). More noticeable, however, are stork nests on chimneys and towers. Continue along riverbank for 3.5km, passing under railway bridge. Turn L away from river, cross level crossing and continue over roundabout on cycle track L beside Rudolf-von-Habsburg-Strasse into **Germersheim** (30km; 105m) (accommodation, refreshments, tourist office, cycle shop, station).

For Leimersheim (1km) (accommodation, refreshments), turn L and follow road into village.

Germersheim (pop. 20,600) is a former military town in Rheinland-Pfalz. Originally part of the Electoral Palatinate, an independent state within the Holy Roman Empire, it was captured and occupied by France during the Thirty Years' War (1618–48) and again in the Napoleonic Wars (1803–15). After the Bavarians reconquered the city in 1814 they

The old barracks at Germersheim, which are now part of the university

commissioned the building of extensive barracks and fortifications, but by the time these were completed in 1855 they were already out of date. Demilitarisation of the Rhineland after the First World War led to most of the fortifications being destroyed. Of the few parts remaining, one holds the German Roads Museum (Deutsches Strassenmuseum), and others provide university accommodation.

Bear R (Zeughausstrasse), passing German Roads Museum R and continue into Bahnhofstrasse. Turn R at roundabout (Rheinbrückenstrasse, cycle track R), pass under multi-blue hued railway bridge and across two more roundabouts, the second of which has a vintage road-roller in middle. Continue under motorway and through industrial area on Hafenstrasse. Where road bends R leaving Germersheim, turn L along flood dyke (sp Speyer). Bear R alongside railway, then dog-leg under bridge to continue on other side. Bear L uphill into **Lingenfeld** (34km) (accommodation, refreshments, station).

Turn first R (Kirschenallee) and L (Friedrich-Ebert-Strasse). Dog-leg R into Berliner Strasse. Look out for easily missed turn R between houses 42 and 44, and follow this over railway bridge. Bear L into Kolpingstrasse parallel with railway. Turn R over level crossing just before station and continue on cycle track L of Speyerer Strasse with Altrhein behind trees R. Where road turns away from river,

The Technikmuseum in Speyer

Speyer Cathedral

fork R on quiet road dropping down onto flood dyke. Pass fishing club and caravan park L. Where road ends, continue R through barrier along flood dyke on asphalt cycle track winding through woods for 2km. At second crossing of paths turn R and continue along dyke, turning L by waterworks, Continue on dyke for 7km with fields L and woods R, turning sharply L to follow old river (although you cannot see it behind trees R). Turn L to join cycle track beside road heading sharply L (Industriestrasse) with airfield runway R. ▶ Turn R, passing round museum, and at T-junction turn L under road bridge on cycle lane R (Geibstrasse). Pass Fest Platz L to reach traffic lights at road junction with Klipfelsau, where you turn L to reach **Speyer** city centre (51km; 97m) (accommodation, refreshments, YH, tourist office, cycle shop, station).

A most incongruous sight welcomes you to Speyer. Set on rooftops high above the Technikmuseum is a full size Lufthansa Boeing 747.

Speyer (pop. 50,000) stands on a small rise above the Rhine, a location chosen by the Romans for a fort as it was one of few riverside places between Mainz and Basel not susceptible to flooding. This locational advantage continued into medieval times when the

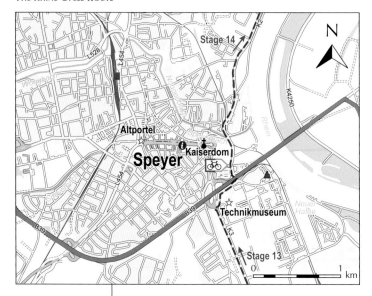

Kaiserdom cathedral (which was Western Europe's largest Romanesque church when it was consecrated in 1061), was built on the same rise. Speyer became an important imperial city within the Holy Roman Empire as the location of the Imperial Chamber of Justice and burial place of eight Emperors.

Power began waning with the Reformation when the cathedral chapter remained Catholic while the city opted for Protestantism. Indeed, the term 'Protestant' derives from 'Protestation of Speyer', a letter of protest presented by German evangelicals to the Imperial Court in 1529, which sealed this split. Other important buildings include the old city gate (Altportel) and the Technikmuseum, which concentrates on transportation technology.

STAGE 14
Speyer to Worms

Start	Klipfelsau, Speyer (97m)
Finish	Ludwigstrasse, Worms (91m)
Distance	49km
Signposting	RR on W bank, local signposting on E bank

This stage starts and ends in historic medieval cities surrounded by agricultural flatlands, with the industrial complex of Mannheim and Ludwigshafen in-between. The BASF plant, which extends 6km alongside the Rhine north of Ludwigshafen, is the world's largest single-company chemical works.

There are three alternative routes through this area. One on the east bank through Mannheim and two on the west bank (both signposted RR), one following the Rhine through Ludwigshafen and one avoiding both cities by passing further west through an open area called Maudacher Bruchwald. This guide mostly follows the western (Ludwigshafen) route, crossing the river temporarily to visit the centre of Mannheim.

From traffic lights at junction with Klipfelsau in **Speyer** continue ahead on cycle track through gardens parallel with Schillerweg, passing below Kaiserdom cathedral L. Pass under pedestrian bridge and follow main road (Hafenstrasse, becoming Franz-Kirrmeier-Strasse) on cycle track L for 6km. Continue ahead at roundabout past waterworks L, with flood dyke R. Follow road as it bears away from Rhine and pass under approach road to single-stay motorway bridge. At Reffenthal (refreshments, camping) where road turns sharply L, leave main road continuing ahead on quiet road. After 150m turn L on asphalt track through fields to reach road again at **Otterstadt** (7km) (accommodation, refreshments, camping).

Turn R and after 50m sharply L on track parallel with flood dyke. Pass caravan park R (behind dyke) and follow dyke as it winds for 7.5km, keeping L below dyke.

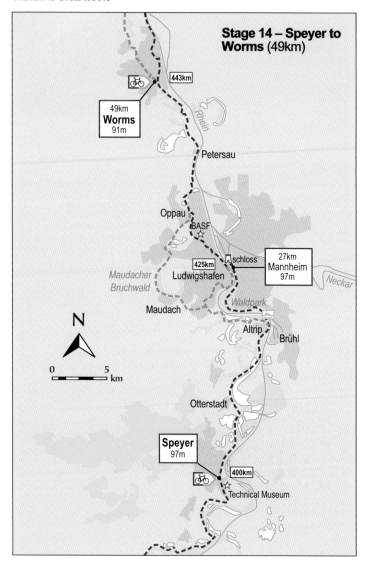

Stage 14 – Worms (49km)

443km

49km
Worms
91m

Rhein

Petersau

Oppau

BASF

425km

schloss

27km
Mannheim
97m

Neckar

Ludwigshafen

Maudacher Bruchwald

Maudach

Waldpark

Altrip

Brühl

N

0   5
km

Otterstadt

Speyer
97m

400km

Technical Museum

Pass another large caravan park L, then join road for 50m before continuing along dyke to reach edge of **Altrip** (14.5km) (accommodation, refreshments, camping). Bear R and continue following flood dyke around village to crossroads with road from village to ferry. Turn R and follow riverside road to **Altrip ferry** (17km).

Cross river to Neckarau and proceed up ferry approach road. Turn L at roundabout (Altriperstrasse) on cycle lane L. Pass first power station (of three) L and turn sharply L at T-junction. Just before entrance to power station turn R (Plinaustrasse) with cycle track R and continue along Aufeldstrasse and Marguerrestrasse. At end of third power station, just before allotments, turn L on asphalt track (Rheinbadweg). Zigzag R and L past oil tanks and ascend onto flood dyke. Turn R alongside Rhine, (cycle track on R, footpath L) with allotments then sporting facilities R. At point where flood dyke and footpath bear R away from river, turn L following gravel cycle track signs into woodland of **Waldpark Nature Reserve** (21km). ▶

Emerge from Waldpark on Stephanienstrasse, with houses above R. Turn L on quiet road (Stephanienufer) and continue through parkland onto Rheinpromenade

Route through Waldpark is complicated but well signposted, with maze of winding tracks to negotiate. Cycle route starts as gravel, then becomes asphalt, heading first W then NW and finally NE.

Schloss Mannheim now houses the university

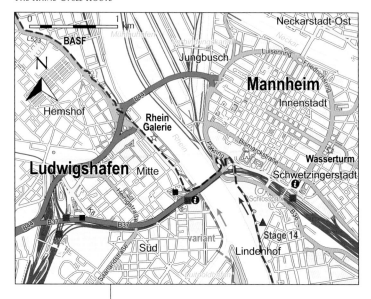

parallel to Rhine with youth hostel R and Konrad Adenauer Bridge ahead. Just past restaurant, fork R (sp Rheinbrücke LU) on cycle track heading under series of five road and rail bridges on approach to crossing of Rhine. Cycle track turns sharply L to reach junction of cycle routes surrounded by slip roads. Turn R to continue over bridge into Ludwigshafen, or L to visit **Mannheim** (27km; 97m) (accommodation, refreshments, YH, tourist office, cycle shop, station). ◄

Turn L, and within 150m arrive at Schloss Mannheim palace. Pass through archway into courtyard and on towards centre of Mannheim.

Mannheim (pop. 313,000) lies at the confluence of the Rhine and Neckar rivers. Unusually for Germany, its city centre streets are laid out in a grid pattern and addresses are given by block rather than using street names. The most noticeable building, Schloss Mannheim palace (completed in 1760), which was home to the Elector Palatinate, now houses the university. The city's symbol, Wasserturm, is an old water tower east of the centre.

Mannheim can justifiably claim to be home to the automobile as Karl Benz produced his first petrol-powered car here (in 1885), and his wife Bertha took the world's first recorded long-distance motor journey, 104km from Mannheim to Pforzheim in 1888. A replica of this first car stands near Wasserturm. The Daimler factory still produces buses and diesel engines.

Turning R, pass under two more bridges then circle R to turn up onto bridge. Cross river on cycle track R of bridge and bear R alongside slip road leading down into **Ludwigshafen** (28km) (accommodation, refreshments, tourist office, cycle shop, station).

Continue on cycle track alongside Lichtenbergerstrasse and Zollhofstrasse passing **Rhein-Galerie** indoor shopping centre on riverbank R. Fork L up towards Kurt-Schumacher-Brücke, drop down R on cycle track under approach roads to bridge and turn R at path junction between slip roads. Continue N alongside main road to reach **BASF** chemical plant and bear L past main entrance. For next 5km cycle track follows alongside this factory R.

The employees' cycle park for company cycles at BASF Ludwigshafen

BASF, headquartered in Ludwigshafen, is the world's largest chemical company. Founded in 1865 as Badische Aniline und Soda Fabrik, the Ludwigshafen factory produced synthetic dyes. In 1913 a new plant was built at Oppau (3km beyond Ludwigshafen) to produce fertilisers. It was here in 1921 that the largest peacetime catastrophe in Germany occurred, when an explosion killed 565 people. The plant was subject to heavy bombing during the Second World War. Subsequent rebuilding and infilling between the two plants to produce plastics has resulted in the world's largest integrated chemical plant (*verbund*) covering 10sq km and employing 32,000 people. Internal transport systems include buses, trains and a fleet of red cycles with silver mudguards.

Continue past BASF visitor centre R at Gate 2 (30km) and bear R (Brunckstrasse). Pass more gates and dog-leg behind a filling station. Bear R again, passing more factory entrances and follow cycle track R and L through bus station. Cross next factory entrance (Gate 13) and soon after extensive bicycle parking R, turn sharply L (Rheinstrasse) away from BASF. Pass under road bridge to reach traffic lights at beginning of **Oppau** (34.5km) (accommodation, refreshments).

Turn R (Ostring) and after 150m R again onto asphalt cycle track into woods. Emerge onto cycle track parallel to main road. At T-junction turn R under road, cross railway and bear R below flood dyke. Turn sharply L parallel to road, with BASF safe harbour (for hazardous cargoes) R. Pass under road, bear R alongside next road and after 150m turn L onto track between fields (Muldenweg). Turn R alongside motorway and where this rises onto red sandstone arches to cross Rhine, turn L under bridge. Continue on asphalt cycle track for 9km, mostly following flood dyke, at first close to Rhine passing waterworks L. After stable complex at **Petersau** L (41km), bear away from river, cross side road and wind ahead beside dyke through fields. Follow flood dyke parallel to road, passing

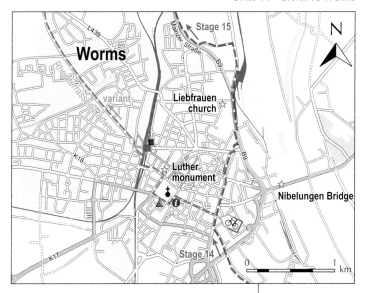

between farm L and open-air theatre R, then turn R and bear L to cross road and continue through fields. At crossing of tracks and dykes turn L and just before reaching road sharply R to head across field on wide asphalt track. Pass car park L and climb up onto dyke. Take first turn L and follow dyke past sports club. Ignore cycle track L, and bear R (Friedrichsweg). Continue through avenue of trees (cycle track L) for 3km to reach outskirts of Worms. Cross bridge over main road and at T-junction turn R (Ludwigstrasse) into **Worms** (49km; 91m) (accommodation, refreshments, YH, camping, tourist office, cycle shop, station). ▶

To reach YH, turn L at first traffic lights (Hagenstrasse) and bear L and R around cathedral.

Having been founded in Roman times, **Worms** (pop. 82,000) claims to be Germany's oldest city (a claim that is disputed by Köln and Trier). The Battle of Worms in 436 was the basis for the German Nibelungen saga. Holy Roman emperor Charlemagne built a palace here and by the 11th century Worms was a prosperous imperial city and

*Nibelungen Bridge
tower at Worms*

scene of several important events in the history of
the Holy Roman Empire, in particular the Edict
of Worms (1521). This declared Martin Luther an
outlaw for failing to recant his reformist beliefs, an
action that led to the eventual establishment of the
Lutheran church.

Important buildings include the cathedral
(another Romanesque masterpiece, although with
later additions it is not complete like Speyer), the
Martin Luther monument (1868) and Nibelungen
Bridge tower. On the northern edge of the town, the
Liebfrauen church stands among vineyards famous
for Liebfraumilch wine.

STAGE 15
Worms to Mainz

Start	Ludwigstrasse, Worms (91m)
Finish	Mainz town hall (86m)
Distance	53km
Signposting	RR

Leaving the industrial suburbs of Worms, the route closely follows the Rhine on new flood dykes looping around on a wide flood plain. It passes through open farming countryside with little forestry, and a low ridge of vineyard-covered hills can be seen to the west. These hills are met at Oppenheim, from where the route continues through vineyards below the ridge to Mainz.

Alternative using Rheinterrassen-Radweg
Between Eichersee and Oppenheim the route is on a rough, often muddy 4wd track, barely suitable for touring cycles. An alternative and more direct route from Worms to Oppenheim can be found by following the signposted Rheinterrassen-Radweg. This starts W of Worms station, heading NW on Von-Steuben-Strasse to pick up a line of vineyard-clad hills just outside city. This ridge is followed N, mostly through vineyards, via **Osthofen**, **Alsheim** and **Guntersblum** to **Oppenheim** after 29.5km.

From **Worms** continue N along Ludwigstrasse, fork L (Wallstrasse) and turn R at T-junction (Berliner Ring). Pass through arch and turn immediately L (Karl-Hofmann-Anlage), following road round in front of houses before turning L alongside main road. Cross main road at next crossing and continue N on cycle track beside road. Church visible behind vineyards L is **Liebfrauenkirche**. Where road bears away L, stay on cycle track bearing R into Hafenstrasse with railway yards R. This is dual carriageway, and at next junction move over to cycle on L carriageway (R carriageway is used for loading vehicles).

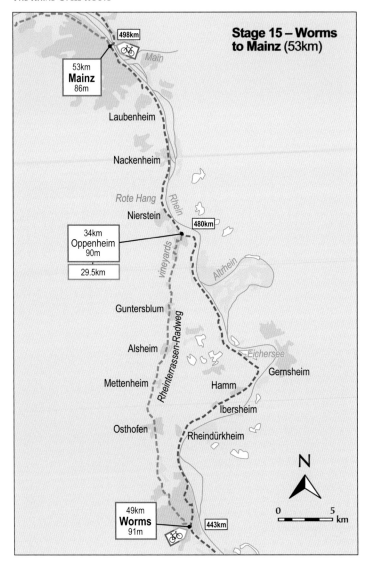

Stage 15 – Worms to Mainz (53km)

498km

53km
Mainz
86m

Laubenheim

Nackenheim

Rote Hang

Rhein

Nierstein

34km
Oppenheim
90m

480km

29.5km

Altrhein

Guntersblum

vineyards

Rheinterrassen-Radweg

Alsheim

Eichersee

Mettenheim

Hamm

Gernsheim

Ibersheim

Osthofen

Rheindürkheim

N

0   5
⊢——————⊣ km

49km
Worms
91m

443km

Opposite flour-mill turn L (Petrus-Dorn-Strasse) and bear R onto cycle track avoiding road junction. Bear R to follow cycle track alongside main road. Continue under railway bridge and turn second R (Im Pfaffenwinkel). Cross road at end and continue ahead along asphalt cycle track with trees L and factory R. Cross railway line and turn L parallel to river. Where road turns L into factory, continue along riverbank and ahead onto asphalt cycle track along flood dyke. Continue beside road and after boat launching ramp R, fork R (Am Fahrt) and where this leaves river, continue along riverbank cycle track past factory L. Bear R onto Rheinuferstrasse past **Rheindürkheim** (9km) (accommodation, refreshments).

Continue out of village past boat memorial L on cycle track L of road. Where this ends, cross road and bear R on asphalt cycle track beside flood dyke winding through fields. Follow this for 4km past **Ibersheim** (13km). Just before Hamm fork R (Landdamm) up onto dyke, passing through edge of **Hamm** (15.5km) (accommodation, refreshments).

Continue through village on quiet road (Landdammstrasse) to reach Rhine where road continues along flood dyke. At crossroads, bear half L on cycle track beside flood dyke. Follow this through fields past new gravel workings R and large *wochenendhausgebeit* (weekend home estate) at **Eichersee** R (20.5km) (refreshments).

Continue on asphalt track alongside new dyke, ignoring cycle route signs R, which use old gravel track beside river. Pass pumping station L, continue to wind through fields, crossing local road and passing poultry farm L. Where track ends beside pumping station, turn R on quiet road leading to riverbank. Turn L on rough gravel track beside river, following this for 6km. Dog-leg around ferry ramp (refreshments, ferry weekends only) and continue along riverbank on rough 4wd track. After short stretch on cobbles past launching ramp, continue following river for 700m, then bear away from river. Follow flood dyke R past Oppenheim *flugplatz* (landing strip) R. Cross road serving landing strip and continue following

To reach old centre of Oppenheim, keep straight on past athletics track, pass under railway and turn L uphill.

flood dyke bearing L through trees. Drop down L onto road (Rheinstrasse) and follow this past waterworks R and school R into **Oppenheim**. ◄ Immediately after athletics track, turn R (Dammstrasse) and L (Fahrstrasse) to reach main road by Oppenheim station (34km; 90m) (accommodation, refreshments, camping, tourist office, station).

Oppenheim (pop. 7000), a wine town and home to the German wine-growing museum, sits on a low ridge overlooking the Rhine. This hill is riddled with Kellerlabyrinth, a labyrinth of cellars and tunnels linking houses together underground. Guided tours, booked through the tourist office, visit approximately 650m of tunnels around the town hall that are largely preserved in their original condition. There are thought to be at least 40km of tunnel, although the exact length is not known. Other sights include the Gothic Katharinenkirche church, which has a fine collection of stained glass.

The Rathaus and Katharinenkirche, Oppenheim

Just before main road turn R on cycle track alongside marina and continue beside busy main road. Follow track R down towards Nierstein ferry, crossing ramp just before Rhine onto cycle track ahead. Continue on cycle track beside road through car park R into **Nierstein** (36.5km) (accommodation, refreshments, tourist office, station). ▶

Sitting below the vineyards of Rote Hang (red slope), **Nierstein** (pop. 7800) is a premier wine town producing mostly white Reisling wine. The town centre is an amalgam of old noble houses and traditional weingüter. The Glöck estate is Germany's oldest recorded vineyard. The parish church of St Kilian sits above town on the side of Rote Hang.

Continue through second car park, and just before end turn L across main road into Rheinstrasse. Pass under railway and turn R (Abtsgasse). At end turn R (Breitgasse) and immediately fork L into Kiliansweg. Parish church can be seen through vineyards L. Continue through vineyards of **Rote Hang**, contouring across hillside for

The wine town of Nierstein

For an attractive diversion through Nierstein passing traditional *weingüter* (wineries), turn L (Dammgasse) under railway and follow signposts R up into old centre. Rejoin main route at junction of Rheinstrasse and Abtsgasse.

Cycle track through vineyards on Rote Hang (red slope), Nierstein

2.5km. Turn R and L to continue beside railway. Where track emerges onto road turn sharply R over level crossing and immediately L onto asphalt cycle track between main road R and railway L. Follow this into **Nackenheim** (41.5km) (refreshments, accommodation).

Where track divides, fork R and continue behind wall dropping down to pass under main road. Turn L and continue out of village on 4wd track along riverbank for 5km, passing new sluices. Dog-leg around riverside campsite and continue on road. Cross ramp to aggregates quay and turn L. After 30m turn sharply R along concrete block track. Pass car park and continue on asphalt cycle track. Turn L by Weisenauer rowing club alongside motorway. Turn R onto cycle track beside road and pass under motorway. Immediately after bridge cross road L and continue between road and railway. Cross two railway sidings and continue alongside cement works R. Continue beside river past Weisenau L and under railway bridge to emerge on cycle track beside marina L. Cross bridge L over marina entrance. Turn R to follow cycle track alongside river past Fort Malakoff L into **Mainz**

(53km; 86m) (accommodation, refreshments, YH, camping, tourist office, cycle shop, station).

Mainz (pop. 199,000), sitting opposite the confluence of the Rhine and Main, was one of the most important religious cities north of the Alps and the only Catholic archbishopric outside Rome designated as a Holy See. A long line of bishops, dating from AD745 to 1802, included Bishop Hatto of Mouse Tower fame (see Stage 16). The Mainzer Dom cathedral of St Martin is over 1000 years old, while the church of St Stephan contains post-war windows by artist Marc Chagall. The huge domed Christuskirche (1898) is the principal Protestant church. Mainz's most famous son is Johannes Gutenberg, inventor of movable type and father of the printing press. A museum records his achievements and the university is named after him.

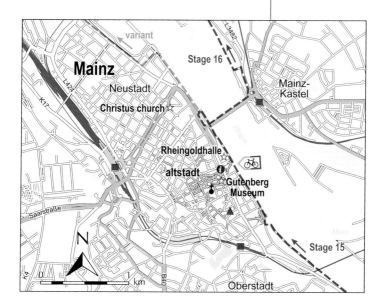

153

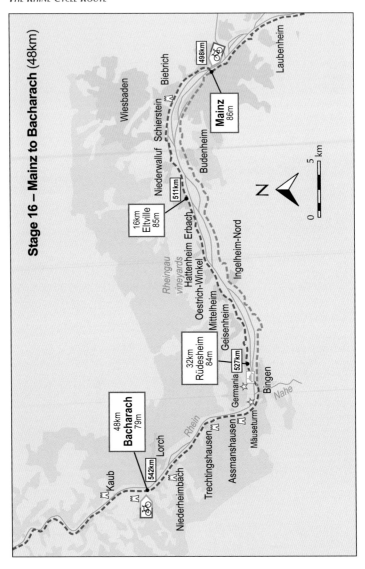

Stage 16 – Mainz to Bacharach (48km)

STAGE 16
Mainz to Bacharach

Start	Mainz town hall (86m)
Finish	Bacharach station (79m)
Distance	48km
Signposting	RR

After an industrial start past Wiesbaden, the flood plains are left behind as the Rhine reaches the ridge formed by the Hunsrück and Taunus mountains. The route follows the east bank of river through Rheingau, passing a series of attractive wine villages below some of Germany's finest vineyards. Crossing over by ferry from Rüdesheim to Bingen, the cycle track closely follows the river as it enters the Rhine Gorge, with castles perched high above vine-covered slopes on both sides of the river.

There are two routes between Mainz and Bingen. This guide follows the more attractive east bank route through the wine-producing villages of the Rheingau. The west bank route is marginally shorter and avoids crossing the river.

Continue N along riverfront in **Mainz** (Uferstrasse) passing modern Rathaus and **Rheingoldhalle** concert hall L. Fork L onto upper level to pass beach area below R and continue under bridge. Turn L through formal gates, cross slip road and turn L up cycle track towards Rhine bridge. Cross river, and bear L alongside first exit road. After 300m, turn L (Rheinufer) through gardens to reach riverside. Turn R on gravel track and continue on road (Eleonorenstrasse). Where road turns away, continue ahead on gravel track, which becomes asphalt, passing apartments R. At end turn R through dirt car park, and L (Biebricher Strasse) to pass under railway bridge. Continue ahead through industrial area onto Rheingaustrasse to reach mini-roundabout. Immediately after roundabout, turn L and R along riverbank to reach Wiesbaden quay in **Biebrich** (6.5km) (accommodation, refreshments, camping, station). ▶

To reach Wiesbaden centre (5km) turn R beside Schloss Biebrich and follow signposted route through palace grounds (Schlossgarten) and on along Biebrich Allee.

Continue along riverbank, and just after Schloss Biebrich palace bear L (Uferstrasse). Moving slightly away from river, pass boat club L. Immediately after campsite turn L into park and R onto winding path parallel with road. Just before motorway bridge, turn R and L under bridge along road used for overnight parking of trucks (Hafenweg). Continue ahead at crossroads and pass between new apartments R and **Schierstein** marina L (9km) (refreshments).

Continue alongside marina on Hafenstrasse, becoming Christian-Bücher-Strasse. Where road turns away, continue ahead, then bear L round swimming club. At end turn L and sharply R up onto flood dyke. Pass waterworks R. ◄ Follow track bearing away from river, then turn L (Werftstrasse) passing artificial football pitch L. Continue on Rheinallee to enter **Niederwalluf** (12.5km) (accommodation, refreshments, station).

This area is a nature reserve and favoured nesting and feeding area for many birds, particularly storks.

Continue past Vereinshaus on concrete block track parallel to river, becoming gravel as it leaves village. Eltville soon comes into view ahead and vineyards appear on slopes R. Pass castellated red Burg Crass Castle and white Kurfürstliche Burg tower to reach **Eltville** (16km; 85m) (accommodation, refreshments, tourist office, cycle shop, station).

Eltville (pop. 17,650) is one of the prettiest towns on the Rhine, and has many attractive wood-frame houses and a large number of roses. The south-facing slopes above the town produce high-quality grapes, enabling local wineries to produce some of Germany's finest wine.

Continue past promenade gardens (Platz von Montrichard) L and Weinhaus Matheus Müller R. At end of village continue along riverbank on asphalt cycle track, passing **Erbach** to reach pretty wine village of **Hattenheim** (20km) (accommodation, refreshments, camping, station).

Bear R and L around cafe, then second L and bear R to circle through car park, before returning to riverbank.

Old riverside crane at Oestrich-Winkel

Continue to **Oestrich-Winkel** (22.5km) (accommodation, refreshments) where there is a renovated 18th-century crane used for loading wine barrels. Powered by two men walking inside a wheel, it was extremely dangerous to operate.

Continue past ferry ramp at **Mittelheim** (24km) (accommodation, refreshments, tourist office, station). Dog-leg away from river around aggregates quay and, after a short section between road and river, bear R away from river on concrete block track winding between woodland L and road R. Turn L onto track coming over footbridge, following this to reach riverbank. Turn R past allotments R and dog-leg behind another aggregates quay at **Geisenheim** (accommodation, refreshments, camping, cycle shop, station).

Continue along riverbank past Fliegerdenkmal (flyers' monument) in gardens R, then campsite R. Turn R away from river and pass between marina L and waterworks R. Turn L alongside main road and after 100m bear L on lower of two tracks. Continue under ruins of Hindenburgbrücke. ▶ Bear L to return to river and pass

This stone arch railway bridge, the second longest over the Rhine, was built in 1915 and destroyed by retreating German forces in 1945.

Rüdesheim, with vineyards and the Germania monument (right) on Weinberg hill

Germania statue in Niederwald near Rüdesheim

R another campsite and swimming pool. Emerge parallel to railway through **Rüdesheim** (32km; 84m) (accommodation, refreshments, YH, camping, tourist office, cycle shop, station).

Rüdesheim, Germany's second most popular destination for foreign tourists after Köln Cathedral, has at its centre Drosselgasse, a narrow street lined with weinstuben, guest houses and tourist shops. Here you can try *eiswein* (a dessert wine made from grapes picked after the first frost has greatly increased sugar levels) or Rüdesheimer coffee (coffee with whipped cream and brandy). Atop the vineyard-clad Weinberg hill (which can be reached by cycle after a tough uphill ride, or by chairlift!) is the Niederwalddenkmal (1883), a gigantic statue of Germania, commemorating the creation of a united Germany after victory in the Franco-Prussian war. Other attractions include Siegfried's Mechanical Music Museum and the Asbach brandy distillery.

Continue between railway and river to landing stage for passenger ferry (for car ferry, continue short distance along road). ▶ Cross river to **Bingen** (34km) (accommodation, refreshments, YH, tourist office, cycle shop, station), where E and W bank routes rejoin.

From car ferry quay proceed up ramp and turn R parallel to railway. Continue for 1.5km alongside new development and riverside gardens R. From passenger ferry go ahead through gardens and turn R to join this route on cycle track parallel to railway. Bear L and R, passing congress hall and museum Strom R, and cross River Nahe. Continue ahead on asphalt cycle track with private park and allotments R. From here you have views of **Mäuseturm** (Mouse Tower) R on island, and Ehrenfels Castle on opposite bank of Rhine.

There are separate passenger and car ferries from Rüdesheim to Bingen; both take cycles.

The **Legend of the Mäuseturm** tells of a rapacious bishop of Mainz, Bishop Hatto, who collected taxes in the form of grain from local peasantry. Every year his demands grew, causing the peasants to complain. The Bishop tricked them to a meeting in

The Mäuseturm at Bingen

one of his barns, saying they were going to receive handouts of grain. When they were inside, the Bishop locked the door and burnt them to death. Only the mice from the barn escaped, and joined by thousands of other mice they pursued the Bishop who fled to the safety of his tower in the river. The mice swam to the tower, caught the Bishop and gnawed him to death. It is said that if you listen closely, his screams can still be heard. The truth is more mundane: the tower was a toll house, built by the Bishop to extract revenue from passing boats.

Past Bingen, river enters Rhine Gorge, with cycle track, road and railway following closely along riverbank until gorge ends just before Koblenz. Continue past woodland R and on along riverside, with considerable amount of Japanese knotweed growing on banks. Pass **Assmanshausen** R on opposite bank and Rheinstein Castle (above L). Cross a metal plate marking 50°N. Just before Trechtingshausen, turn L and R around caravan park then follow railway beneath Reichenstein Castle L and through allotments into **Trechtingshausen** (40.5km) (accommodation, refreshments, camping, station).

Continue along riverbank, passing **Niederheimbach** (45.5km) L with **Lorch** opposite R. Pass below Fürstenberg Castle L, and just before Bacharach, fork L uphill to emerge alongside main road. Follow cycle track alongside road, above campsite, to **Bacharach** station (48km; 79m) (accommodation, refreshments, YH, camping, tourist office, cycle shop, station).

STAGE 17
Bacharach to Koblenz

Start	Bacharach station (79m)
Finish	Deutsches Eck, Koblenz (65m)
Distance	50km
Signposting	RR

This stage offers spectacular scenery as the river forges its way through the Rhine Gorge between the Hunsrück and Taunus mountain ranges, accompanied by road, railway and cycle track. A series of pretty riverside towns are passed, including St Goar with the famous Loreley Rock nearby. The gorge sides are covered by vineyards and forest, with numerous romantic castles standing sentinel above. The gorge ends just before the military city of Koblenz. Most of the route is on good-quality cycle tracks along the riverside.

Continue through **Bacharach** on cycle track alongside main road. If you have visited town centre, cross railway and turn N on main road. Burg Stahleck Castle, looking like a space rocket, sits above town L. Cycle track runs between road L and river R for 6km, passing beautifully restored Pfalzgrafenstein Castle on an island just before **Kaub** village and Gutenfels Castle (nowadays a hotel) on opposite bank. Pass below Schönburg Castle (another hotel) L and arrive at **Oberwesel** (7km) (accommodation, refreshments, YH, tourist office, cycle shop, station).

Pass behind filling station, continuing through village on cycle track beside road. Where track forks, keep L alongside road. Continue for 4.5km to pass most famous sight of the entire Rhine, **Loreley** (Lorelei) Rock, on opposite bank R (accommodation, refreshments, camping). ▸

To visit Loreley, cross ferry from St Goar to St Goarshausen, cycle along riverbank past maiden's statue and, leaving cycle at bottom of cliff, follow footpath to summit.

The **Loreley Rock** is a sheer promontory jutting out from the east bank of the Rhine, forcing the river to make a sharp turn. The cliffs are 120m high with a viewpoint and restaurant on top. Beneath the cliff,

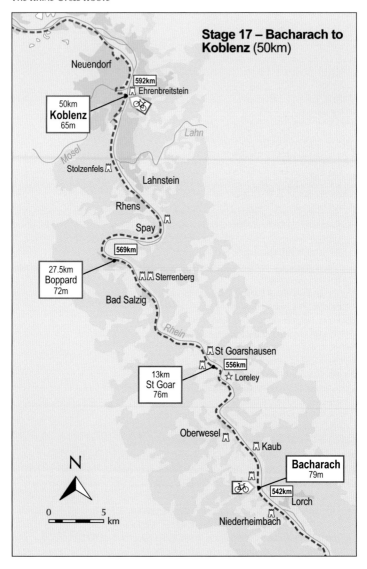

Stage 17 – Bacharach to Koblenz (50km)

Neuendorf

592km
Ehrenbreitstein

50km
Koblenz
65m

Stolzenfels

Lahnstein

Rhens

Spay

569km

27.5km
Boppard
72m

Sterrenberg

Bad Salzig

Rhein

St Goarshausen

556km

13km
St Goar
76m

☆ Loreley

Oberwesel

Kaub

Bacharach
79m

542km

Lorch

Niederheimbach

N

0   5
━━━━━━━━ km

the river bend is partly obstructed by underwater rocks, leaving a narrow navigable channel with treacherous currents.

The legend of Loreley is of a fair maiden who, having been spurned by her fisherman boyfriend, swore vengeance upon all riverfarers. She sat atop the cliff singing alluring songs to lure them towards the rocks and their doom. Nowadays, although the river has been dredged, these are still dangerous waters and larger boats take on a pilot to navigate past the Loreley. A bronze statue of the siren, marked by a flag, sits at the end of a long narrow spit just downstream of the rock.

Passing Loreley, stay on upper level beside road, with campsite below R, and soon reach ferry at beginning of **St Goar** (13km; 76m) (accommodation, refreshments, YH, camping, tourist office, station).

Cycle through St Goar on cycle track through riverside gardens R. Where gardens end, roadside cycle track resumes and continues past marina R with Burg Rheinfels Castle above L. Katz Castle sits above **St Goarshausen** on opposite bank. Continue along cycle track passing

The Loreley Rock in the Rhine Gorge

163

another marina at Fellen and Maus Castle across river. Continue past Hirzenach to reach **Bad Salzig** (23km) (accommodation, refreshments).

The two castles of **Sterrenberg and Liebenstein** feature in a legend of two brothers, sons of the lord of Sterrenberg, and their cousin Angela, who came to live with them when her father died. Both brothers were attracted to Angela. Henry, the restrained elder brother, kept his feelings secret, while his impetuous sibling Conrad wooed and won her hand. Before the couple could marry, the Crusaders passed by recruiting volunteers to fight the Turks. Conrad went away to war, leaving Henry to look after his fiancée. Years passed and the old lord built a second castle, Liebenstein, across a narrow defile from Sterrenberg, as a home for his younger son and niece when they married.

Eventually, the war was over and Conrad returned, accompanied by a Grecian princess he had married while he was away. Henry was furious and challenged his brother to a duel, but Angela came between them, urging them not to fight over her. She then went off to become a nun. Henry had a wall built between the castles so he should not see Conrad. After a cold winter in Germany, the Grecian princess fled south with a passing knight. Grief-stricken, Conrad threw himself from the battlements and died. Both castles still stand, with the wall between them as testimony to this tragic tale.

Continue on cycle track between road and river past **Sterrenberg** and Liebenstein castles opposite R. Opposite Kamp, cycle track leaves road, dropping down R following river. Pass *senfmühle* (mustard mill) and underneath sports clubhouse on quiet residential street (Rheinallee). Continue past gardens and ferry R onto cycle track along **Boppard** promenade (27.5km; 72m) (accommodation, refreshments, camping, tourist office, cycle shop, station). ◄

To reach centre of walled town of Boppard, with many attractive half-timbered houses, turn L into Kronen-Gasse.

At end of Boppard promenade, where road bears L, fork R following cycle track alongside river. Pass large semi-circular residential buildings L, following white arrows on road and turn L away from river at next junction. Turn R on cycle track alongside main road following river around 180 degrees. On this stretch, extensive vineyards cover gorge sides L. Follow road passing above Sonneneck campsite R, then immediately after campsite fork R (sp Spay), ignoring cycle track ahead which bypasses Spay. Turn R beside Peter's chapel (Rheinufer) and L onto asphalt cycle track between allotments L and meadows R. Continue on quiet road into **Spay** (35km) (accommodation, refreshments, station).

The walled town of Boppard

A marker stone in **Spay** indicates the halfway point along the navigable river between Basel and Rotterdam (414km each way). There are many pretty red-and-white *fachwerkhäuser* (half-timbered buildings), including one with flood marks showing the highest flood (in 1882) 3m above the flood dyke, and recent floods including those of 1993 and 1995, which reached close to this level.

Continue onto Holgertsweg, passing a large factory (Schottel) producing rudder propellers for boats. Where track splits, bear R along riverside out of Spay and continue with Marksburg Castle above Braubach on opposite bank. Pass between boat ramp and campsite L and continue along riverside, with railway L, past **Rhens** station (39.5km) (tourist office, station).

Continue ahead onto Am Rhein, passing Königsstuhl hotel and boat pier R. Route bears gently L away from river through allotments and continues on red brick-block track into Brunnerstrasse, which becomes cobbled. Pass Rhenser mineral water factory R, where a drinking fountain runs with naturally carbonated mineral water. Where road turns L away from river, continue ahead past beer garden on riverbank. Just before end of Brunnerstrasse, turn R between houses and L on cycle track along riverbank, with views of Lahnstein opposite. Pass below **Stolzenfels Castle** L, the best preserved of all Rhine castles, and continue between railway and river. Soon after passing Königsbacher brewery L, bear L up onto flood dyke and continue on gravel track under trees. Pass under motorway and railway bridges, through barrier and ahead into Koblenz along residential

The fortress of Ehrenbreitstein opposite Koblenz

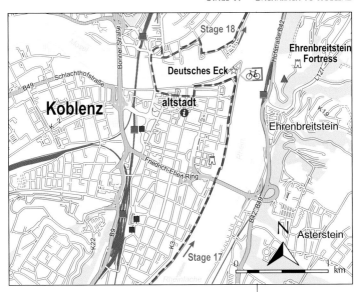

street (Rheinau). Turn L into a crescent (Beethovenstrasse) and continue across roundabout into Mozartstrasse. Cross bridge over marina and immediately bear R downhill on asphalt track. Turn R on concrete block track through gardens, then dog-leg L and continue past statue of Empress Kaiserin Augusta L. Pass Weindorf restaurant complex L, continuing under Pfaffendorferbrücke bridge and through gardens (landscaped for German national gardening festival in 2011) between Residenzschloss Electoral Palace L and river. After a series of landing stages arrive at **Deutsches Eck** (German Corner), the point where Mosel and Rhine rivers meet in the middle of **Koblenz** (50km; 65m) (accommodation, refreshments, YH, camping, tourist office, cycle shop, station).

> Originally founded by the Romans, **Koblenz** (pop. 106,000) was the seat of the archbishop and prince elector of Trier from 1018 until 1794. Fought over and occupied by the French on a number of

The Mosel (left) joins the Rhine (right) at Deutsches Eck in Koblenz

occasions, the city became part of Prussia after the Congress of Vienna in 1815. The city was heavily fortified, centring on Ehrenbreitstein citadel overlooking the city from the east bank of the Rhine. The city's most famous monument, a 14m-high equestrian statue of Kaiser Wilhelm I, was erected at Deutsches Eck in 1897. Destroyed by US artillery in 1945, the pieces were kept and eventually recast, finally being reinstated to celebrate German reunification in 1993. The riverside gardens between the palace and Deutsches Eck were landscaped and linked across the Rhine by cable car to Ehrenbreitstein as part of the German national gardening festival in 2011.

STAGE 18
Koblenz to Königswinter

Start	Deutsches Eck, Koblenz (65m)
Finish	Königswinter ferry (54m)
Distance	59km
Signposting	RR (and D8 from Bad Honnef)

As the gorge widens out, the River Rhine continues through a narrow valley, with mountains never far away. This area has been subject to volcanic activity in the past, as can be seen at an active geyser close to Andernacht. This stage of the route follows cycle tracks, usually close to the river, along the west bank, before crossing the river at Rolandseck to end at the resort town of Königswinter immediately below the Drachenfels mountains.

From Deutsches Eck in **Koblenz**, follow Peter-Altmeier-Ufer away from Rhine, parallel with Mosel. Turn second L (Kornpfortstrasse) and R (Auf der Danne becoming Florinsmark, then Burgstrasse) through old town. Continue ahead to reach bridge over Mosel. Turn R to cross river on cycle track beside road, and follow road round R on N side of river. Turn R (Gartenstrasse) and L (Neuendorferstrasse), continuing past flood dyke R. Turn R (sp Sportsplatz) into Schartwiesenweg and follow this bearing L between football pitch L and shipyards R. Pass campsite R and continue ahead (Am Ufer) between allotments L and grassy open space R, eventually reaching Rhine in **Neuendorf** (4km) (accommodation, refreshments).

Bear R on new road along flood dyke behind houses L. Where this ends, continue ahead out of village on asphalt cycle track beside river. Pass sewerage works and turn L (Fritz-Ludwig-Strasse), crossing two level crossings. At end, turn R on cycle track alongside Hans-Böckler-Strasse passing through aluminium works. Turn R at roundabout (Carl-Spaeter-Strasse) and bear L

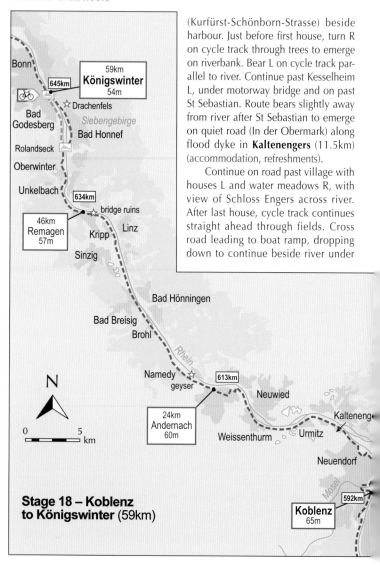

Stage 18 – Koblenz to Königswinter (59km)

(Kurfürst-Schönborn-Strasse) beside harbour. Just before first house, turn R on cycle track through trees to emerge on riverbank. Bear L on cycle track parallel to river. Continue past Kesselheim L, under motorway bridge and on past St Sebastian. Route bears slightly away from river after St Sebastian to emerge on quiet road (In der Obermark) along flood dyke in **Kaltenengers** (11.5km) (accommodation, refreshments).

Continue on road past village with houses L and water meadows R, with view of Schloss Engers across river. After last house, cycle track continues straight ahead through fields. Cross road leading to boat ramp, dropping down to continue beside river under

railway bridge. Pass **Urmitz** (13.5km) (accommodation, refreshments) on cycle track between village and river. Cross another boat ramp and pass closed Mülheim Kärllich nuclear power station L. Emerge onto quiet road by small quay and continue alongside flood dyke past **Weissenthurm** (18km) (accommodation, refreshments, station).

The Runde Turm, Andernach, built in 1453 as part of the medieval city fortifications

Leave village on cycle track under motorway bridge and move slightly away from river passing small harbour R, with view of Neuwied opposite. Continue along riverbank, crossing a sidestream, to reach quiet road on top of flood dyke L. Bear R along this road to reach a road junction. Turn L away from river, on cycle track beside road and follow this round end of harbour. Pass port offices R and turn L on multi-use track beside Hans-Julius-Ahlmann-Strasse, passing entrance to Rasselstein steel rolling mills L. Where road bears L, keep straight ahead on cycle track between Macdonalds L and cemetery R. Turn R onto multi-use track alongside Koblenzer Strasse and follow this, crossing number of side streets, to reach city walls and gatehouse of **Andernach** (24km; 60m) (accommodation, refreshments, tourist office, station).

Cold water geyser at Namedyer Werth, Andernach

Andernach (pop. 29,500) city centre is surrounded by the remnants of medieval city walls, with a number of restored towers and gates. In Namedyer Werth, 1.5km downstream from Andernach but reached by boat from a visitor centre on the riverside promenade, is the world's highest cold water geyser. The geyser started in 1903 when a borehole drilled for mineral water extraction was discovered to erupt at regular intervals. Over time, pressure dropped as other holes were drilled, with eruptions ceasing in 1953. A new borehole in 2001 reactivated the geyser, and it was subsequently opened to visitors. Eruptions of cold water driven by carbon dioxide reach 64m high and occur at approximately two-hourly intervals.

Turn R parallel with city walls (Hindenburgwall). At end, follow cycle track across junction and turn L along cycle track beside promenade (Konrad-Adenauer-Allee). Pass visitor centre for Andernach geyser L, continuing beside promenade to point where it turns away from river. Turn R and immediately L through riverside gardens. Just before preserved crane, turn L, cross road then zigzag under railway. Turn R, steeply uphill, and continue beneath motorway viaduct with railway L. When viaduct ends, cycle track emerges on L of motorway, soon following railway to join residential street (Hauptstrasse) through **Namedy** (28km) (accommodation, station).

Continue out of village through fields, passing Schloss Namedy L. Zigzag under railway and continue parallel with motorway R into start of Brohl. Pass industrial units L, and turn L by last building. Turn L and R at complicated junction beside Brohl station and continue parallel to slip road from overbridge. Turn R under bridge and L to rejoin Koblenzer Strasse. Cross level crossing and continue beside main road through **Brohl** (32.5km) (refreshments, station).

Old milestone in Brohl showing distances in Prussian miles (1 mile = 7.5km)

Pass beginning of harbour R, and turn L into side street beside Brohler Quellen mineral water factory. After 50m, turn L down slope to pass under railway and R up other side. At top of slope turn sharply L and immediately R onto Artilleriestrasse. Continue on road through woods to reach another complicated junction at Wagrambrücke. At junction keep R ahead and immediately turn R on cycle track zigzagging down into gorge. Pass under railway and main road and turn L over stream. Continue through a field and onto ferry ramp. Just before ferry, bear L on cycle track parallel to Rhine. Continue along riverside, with houses set back L, to reach promenade through centre of **Bad Breisig** (36km) (accommodation, refreshments, camping, tourist office, cycle shop, station).

Where promenade ends, continue along cycle track beside river for 6km through hay meadows of Goldene Miele. Cross River Ahr on small, covered wooden bridge to reach road by village of **Kripp** (42km) (accommodation, refreshments).

Follow cycle track to reach ferry ramp, with view of Linz opposite. Join road and where this ends, continue on cycle track beside river for 2.5km, past campsite L, to reach ruins of Ludendorff (Remagen) railway bridge. Continue along traffic-free promenade to emerge on road in **Remagen** (46km; 57m) (accommodation, refreshments, camping, tourist office, station).

> **Ludendorff Bridge** at Remagen (built in 1916) was the only Rhine bridge captured intact by advancing Allied forces in March 1945. Attempts to demolish it by German sappers failed and four officers were subsequently court-martialled and shot. However, the bridge had been weakened, and 10 days later it collapsed suddenly, killing 28 American army engineers. During this period a substantial bridgehead was established on the east bank and pontoon bridges projected across the river enabled the Allied advance to continue despite the bridge's collapse. Bridge towers remain on both banks, the one on the west bank containing a peace museum and memorial.

Continue through pedestrian precinct on riverfront promenade in Remagen. ▶ When promenade ends, continue on cycle track between railway and river for 3km. Where railway turns away from river, continue along riverbank, passing below houses at **Unkelbach** to emerge onto road just before **Oberwinter** (51km) (accommodation, refreshments).

On the hill ahead is Apollinaris church, famous for murals painted by artist group called the 'Nazarenes'.

Follow cycle track alongside road (Bonnerstrasse) through village, passing marina R. Continue past boatyard and turn R into easily missed alley. This zigzags to reach river. Turn L along riverbank to reach ferry ramp at **Rolandseck** (53km).

The small community of **Rolandseck** has a large, historically significant railway station. Opened in 1858 on an extension of the Köln to Bonn railway, it was a riverside terminus providing connection with Rhine steamships. Provision was lavish, with dining room and function rooms, and attracted the cream of society, including Queen Victoria, Kaiser Wilhelm and Bismarck. Franz Liszt gave concerts in the function room and George Bernhard Shaw wrote in rooms above the station.

After the Second World War, the station closed, and in 1958 plans were made to demolish the building and replace it with smaller facilities. This was resisted and it reopened as a cultural centre and art gallery. Subsequent redevelopment has seen the building restored to its 1906 condition and a new art gallery has been built above the station.

Cross Rhine to **Bad Honnef** (54.5km) (accommodation, refreshments, YH, camping, tourist office, cycle shop, station), and turn L halfway up ferry ramp onto gravel cycle track winding through trees. Pass factory R, to emerge on road (Lohfelder Strasse). Follow cycle lane on pavement L of road, proceeding up bridge ramp and bearing L at top to descend along Rheinpromenade without crossing bridge. Just before second bridge, dog-leg R and continue into forecourt of U-bahn terminus. Take

Königswinter, with Drachenfels rising behind

cycle track running between platforms L and car park R and continue with U-bahn L and tennis club R. Dog-leg R under two pedestrian bridges, and immediately after second, turn R away from U-bahn and L to run alongside railway. Emerge onto quiet road (Karl-Broel-Strasse) and follow this to bus turning circle by Rhöndorf U-bahn station. Continue on cycle track between railway R and U-bahn L. Just before reaching main road, bear L to cross U-bahn, and R onto riverside cycle track. Follow this into **Königswinter** (59km; 54m) (accommodation, refreshments, tourist office, station).

Sitting above Königswinter is **Drachenfels** (Dragon's Rock; 321m), the westernmost peak of the Siebengebirge range of volcanic hills. The name is derived from an episode in the Nibelung saga in which Siegfried slays a cave-dwelling dragon on this hill. The summit has a ruined castle with extensive views south down the Rhine Valley and north to Köln in the far distance. The summit can be reached on foot (2km) – it is too steep to cycle – or by mountain railway. Part way up, the route passes the Nibelungenhaus gallery, which contains paintings depicting scenes from Wagner operas, and Schloss Drachenburg, built in 1884 as a home for a wealthy banker but now owned by the local municipality.

STAGE 19

Königswinter to Köln

Start	Königswinter ferry (54m)
Finish	Köln railway bridge (42m)
Distance	46km
Signposting	RR and D8 (inconsistent) and local signage

Crossing back to the west bank, the route follows the river past Bonn, former capital of West Germany. Between Bonn and Köln, although the landscape is basically industrial with a number of large chemical works, there is plenty of open country. Entry to Köln is along old quays that have been modernised to form attractive new offices, shops and apartments. The terrain is mostly flat.

Catch ferry from ramp in centre of **Königswinter** to **Bad Godesberg** (accommodation, refreshments, station). Turn R along cycle track beside Rhine (John-J-McCloy-Ufer). ▶ Pass Rheinhotel Dreesen L, continue into Von-Sandt-Ufer and cross ferry ramp of Niederdollendorf ferry.

> Across the river is a view of wooded Petersberg hill behind Königswinter, topped by the former official guest residence of the West German government.

> **Rheinhotel Dreesen** was a favourite with Adolf Hitler, who visited over 70 times. It was here he met British Prime Minister Neville Chamberlain in September 1938, prior to signing the Munich Agreement – which promised, according to Chamberlain, 'peace in our time'. Twelve months later, Britain was at war with Germany.

Follow riverbank past residential area L, to reach car turning circle. For next 3km route runs alongside Rheinenaue park L, with on opposite bank major new development on old cement works site. Continue under motorway bridge, still in park. Sandstone **tower** L is monument to Otto von Bismarck (1815–98), German chancellor regarded as father of unified Germany. Cycle track becomes Stresemannufer. Just behind park L are

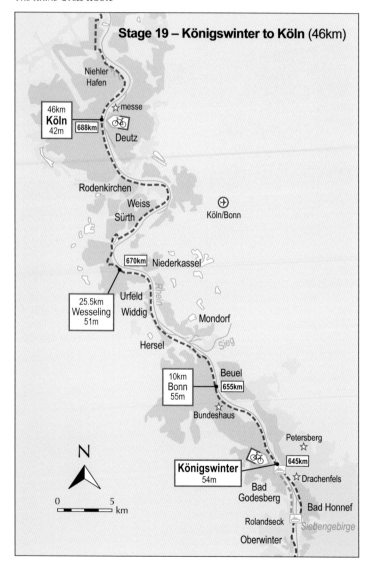

Stage 19 – Königswinter to Köln (46km)

Niehler Hafen

☆ messe

Köln 46km
42m
688km
Deutz

Rodenkirchen

Weiss

Sürth

Köln/Bonn ⊕

670km Niederkassel

Urfeld
25.5km
Wesseling
51m
Widdig

Mondorf

Hersel

Sieg

10km Bonn 55m — Beuel
655km

☆ Bundeshaus

Petersberg ☆

Königswinter
54m
645km

☆ Drachenfels

Bad Godesberg

Bad Honnef

Rolandseck

Siebengebirge

Oberwinter

N

0 — 5 km

The Bundeshaus in Bonn, the former West German parliament building

modernistic glass Deutsches Post tower (tallest building in Nordrhein-Westfalen and headquarters of German post office), slightly lower UN complex and **Bundeshaus** (which housed the West German parliament from 1949–1990, and the German parliament from 1990–1999), now a conference centre. Track continues along river with buildings above high wall L to reach road (Rheinauufer) and **Alter Zoll** quayside in **Bonn** (10km; 55m) (accommodation, refreshments, YH, tourist office, cycle shop, station). ▸

To reach central Bonn, turn L uphill after Alter Zoll (before Kennedybrücke) onto Rheingasse.

From 1949 to 1990, **Bonn** (pop. 325,000) was capital of West Germany, and site of both houses of parliament, presidential offices and most ministries and government departments. Since the capital of reunified Germany moved to Berlin, many of Bonn's former government buildings have found a new lease of life as home for international organisations (including 17 UN institutions) and international conferences.

The composer Ludwig van Beethoven (1770–1827) was born and educated in Bonn, although he moved permanently to Vienna in 1792. His birthplace in Bonngasse, near Marktplatz, can be visited. Statues abound and Beethovenhalle concert hall is named in his honour.

Beethoven's statue in Bonn

Cycle track continues beside road, past opera house L and under Kennedybrücke bridge onto Erzbergerufer. Pass Beethovenhalle concert hall L, and where road bears L, continue ahead on cycle track parallel with river. Pass Römerbad swimming pool complex L, continue under motorway bridge and after 400m (just before loading gantry) turn L away from river. Turn R (Karl-Legien-Strasse) and dog-leg L and R past main entrance of container terminal. Continue ahead following road winding alongside terminal R, then turn R back to riverbank. Follow cycle track into open country to reach Hersel–Mondorf ferry ramp. 250m after ferry ramp, turn L away from river, then R onto cycle track between fields (Auenweg). Fork R (still on Auenweg) and continue past football pitch R to reach **Hersel** (17.5km) (refreshments, station).

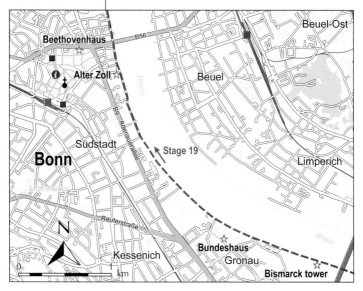

Continue ahead, avoiding village, to regain riverbank and continue for 3km passing Uedorf and **Widdig** (19km) (refreshments, station).

After Widdig, cycle track turns steeply up L onto flood dyke and continues parallel with river as gravel track. Cross boat ramp and continue along riverside on asphalt track passing **Urfeld** (21km) (refreshments, station).

Continue through woods parallel with river, passing between chemical works at Niederkassel R on opposite bank, and Shell Wesseling petro-chemical complex behind trees L. Track veers away from river to pass between oil loading quay R and storage tanks L. Bear gently R towards river, climb up onto flood dyke, cross boat ramp and continue along asphalt track on top of dyke into **Wesseling** (25.5km; 51m) (accommodation, refreshments, station).

Pass KD cruise line pier and ticket kiosk R and turn L (Uferstrasse). Turn R onto main road (Kölner Strasse) and follow this bearing L through town centre. Turn L (Mühlenweg) and R at traffic lights to follow cycle track alongside main road for 2.5km passing through chemical works. Pass Godorf station R, and after 250m, where cycle track ends, cross at traffic lights to L of road. Continue along Industriestrasse for 500m, passing under pipe bridge and climbing up other side. Opposite cooling tower of Shell oil refinery L, turn R (Mühlenhof) and follow road as it bends R to cross railway and bears L. Pass end of harbour and turn R onto cycle track that crosses railway and leads down to Rhine. Turn L at end and immediately fork R along lower level through trees beside river. Continue for 2.5km to cross boat ramp and pass below **Sürth** (32.5km) (accommodation, refreshments, station).

Follow track along riverbank below 5m high wall protecting Sürth from flood waters, and continue past **Weiss**, Weiss–Zündorf ferry R and campsite L, into open country. Where track forks, cycle track bears L (pedestrians bear R) and continues through woods for 2km. Both tracks come together for 100m, then cycle track bears L again to emerge from woods beside entrance to campsite. Turn L and bear R onto cycle path beside road. Pass caravan park R and just before beginning of built-up area, drop down R off flood dyke following cycle track to riverbank. After 1km, track climbs back onto flood dyke and bears R along riverside track to **Rodenkirchen** (40km) (accommodation, refreshments, camping).

Continue under motorway bridge and across boat ramp to join broad cycle track alongside riverbank for 1.6km. Where track divides, fork R remaining close to river and pass under Köln south railway bridge. ◄

Left fork up ramp beside Schönhauser U-bahn station leads to alternative route into Köln centre following cycle track alongside main road.

Next 1.5km, between south railway bridge and Severinsbrücke road bridge, was lined by old riverside warehouses and quays. These have been subject to extensive redevelopment into offices, shops and apartments, with new cycle track created along riverside. Continue past this development and bear L under road bridge to pass German Olympic Museum and **Chocolate Museum** (both R). After short cobbled section, bear L over swing bridge. Turn R on red cycle lane alongside main road. Where this descends into tunnel, bear R passing under Deutzer Brücke bridge onto riverside promenade in centre of **Köln** (46km; 42m) (accommodation, refreshments, YH, camping, tourist office, cycle shop, station).

Quayside development in Köln

Köln Cathedral and Hohenzollern railway bridge

KÖLN

Köln (pop. 1,007,000), the largest city on the Rhine, was founded in 38BC. It became Roman Colonia city (AD50) and provincial capital in AD85, with a population of over 30,000. Many Roman antiquities are housed in the Romano-Germanic Museum. Conversion of the Romans to Christianity led to the appointment of the first bishop in the fourth century. Subsequent prince-bishops and archbishops controlled Köln until 1288 when, after defeat in battle, the Archbishop was expelled from Köln and moved to Bonn.

Control then passed to merchants and guild members, and construction of a great new cathedral started. This was designed to express the city's wealth and house its religious relics, in particular the Ark of the Magi, allegedly containing the bones and clothing of the Three Wise Men. Building continued until the mid-16th century, then ceased with the cathedral only half-finished. The main reasons for this were population decline due to plague, the growth of German Protestantism and a shortage of funds. The unfinished cathedral dominated the Köln skyline for nearly 400 years until 1842 when, with the city prospering again during the industrial revolution, work resumed to original plans. Completed in 1880, it became the world's tallest building for a few years before being supplanted by the Eiffel Tower. ▶

Despite heavy bombing during the Second World War (Köln was the target for the first 1000 bomber raid), which caused considerable damage, the cathedral was not destroyed. Post-war repairs were completed in 1956. However, weathering and pollution mean that restoration is permanently on-going and there is always scaffolding somewhere on the building.

The city's other attractions include a number of breweries in the old town, brewing local kölsch-style beer.

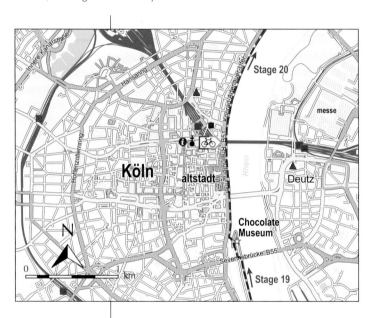

STAGE 20
Köln to Düsseldorf

Start	Köln railway bridge (42m)
Finish	Schlossturm, Düsseldorf (35m)
Distance	52km
Signposting	RR and D8 (both inconsistent), plus local signage

The route traverses what is mainly an industrial area between the great industrial cities of Köln, Leverkusen and Düsseldorf. There is, however, a surprising amount of open country as the river makes wide meanders across the flat plain.

Follow riverside promenade N from **Köln** centre passing KD cruise line quays and ticket office. Pass under railway bridge and just before blue tent-like Musical Dome L, bear L through a gap in wall separating promenade from Konrad-Adenauer-Ufer. Continue along cycle track parallel with road for 2km, passing **Köln Messe** (exhibition centre) on opposite bank and going under Zoobrücke bridge and cable car linking zoo with exhibition centre. Opposite junction with Tiergartenstrasse L, turn R descending below flood dyke and L along cycle track on lower level with water meadows R. After 500m, bear L back onto flood dyke and continue, mostly under trees for 3.5km, passing under Mülheimer Brücke then running parallel to Am Molenkopf L with container terminal of Köln **Niehler Hafen** harbour behind (6.5km).

Continue up ramp and over bridge L at harbour entrance. Turn R on cycle track parallel with road (Niehler Damm), passing gardens R and continuing alongside Rhine with vast Ford plant ahead. Turn L (Bremerhavener Strasse) on cycle track R and just before railway crossing, turn R (Emdener Strasse) following cycle track R of road. Pass Geestemündener Strasse U-bahn station L and continue on cycle track between tram lines

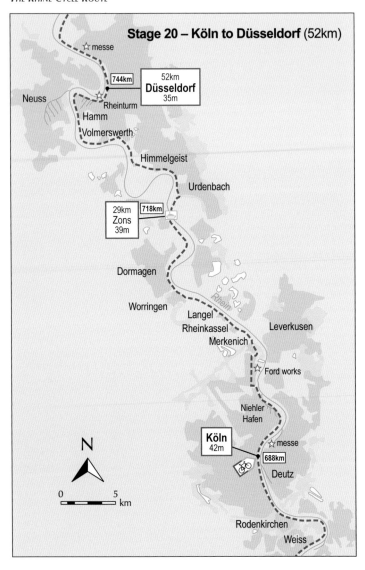

Stage 20 – Köln to Düsseldorf (52km)

R and road L. For next 2km, route runs alongside **Ford motorworks** R. Just before Fordwerke Mitte U-bahn station, dog-leg R across tram tracks, and dog-leg back L after Fordwerke Nord station. Pass under pipe bridge and turn R (Ivenshofweg) at end of factory. At T-junction turn L (Merkenich Hauptstrasse) and follow this through **Merkenich** (12km) (refreshments).

Just before end of village, fork R (Kasselberger Weg), through cutting in flood dyke, under motorway bridge and ahead through fields finally clear of Köln. Where road turns sharply L, continue ahead along flood dyke, passing **Rheinkassel** L (14.5km) (accommodation, refreshments).

At end of village, continue on flood dyke past **Langel** (16km). Drop down R off flood dyke and after 250m reach Langel–Hitdorf ferry ramp. Turn L away from river and after 100m, turn R on asphalt cycle track along flood dyke through fields for 3km with Dormagen chemical works visible ahead. At end, bear R to join road passing **Worringen** L (20.5km) (accommodation, refreshments).

Cross to multi-use track L of road at beginning of village and follow this past Ineos/Bayer chemical works L,

The medieval town of Zons

becoming Kölner Strasse. At traffic lights at end of factory (opposite An der Römerziegelei), turn R across road and L for 100m, then bear diagonally R away from road on flood dyke across water meadows. At road junction just before sewerage works L, move L of road for 200m, then cross dyke and follow below R for 1.25km. Zigzag back up onto dyke at crossroads and continue for 4km to reach T-junction beside medieval **Zons** (29km; 39m) (accommodation, refreshments, tourist office). ◀

To visit Zons, turn L upon reaching road and pass through toll house tower into old town.

> In 1372 the Prince-Bishop of Köln built a toll house and customs building beside the Rhine at **Zons** (pop. 5500). A small walled town developed (now the finest remaining in Nordrhein), with the Friedstrom Fortress to defend it. This survived the Thirty Years' War. However, in the 18th century heavy floods altered the river course so it no longer flowed past the town and Zons' prosperity declined. The fortress ruins contain a museum and archive, and there is open-air theatre in summer.

Turn R at road and R again to reach Zons ferry. Cross Rhine and turn L at top of ramp on quiet road winding through fields with widely spaced mature trees. Turn L at main road (Baumberger Weg) following cycle track L over bridge and into **Urdenbach** (31.5km) (accommodation, refreshments).

Bear L at traffic lights (Am Alten Rhein), passing village R, and follow road to reach riverbank at end of village. Continue alongside river (Benrather Schlossufer) and where road turns away from river continue on riverside cycle track. Bear L alongside main road (Bonnerstrasse), with cycle track L and turn L (Am Trippelsberg) at next crossroads, cycling on road. Pass steel mills, cross railway and continue past other industrial units. Continue winding past fields R, bear L by bus turning circle into Itter and straight over at crossroads (Am Broichgraben). Follow this, turning sharply R then winding through residential area to crossroads. Turn L (Am Steinebrück) into **Himmelgeist** (37.5km) (refreshments).

At T-junction turn R (Steinkaul) and continue ahead (Am Bärenkamp). This becomes Himmelgeister Landstrasse as it leaves village to wind through fields. Where road starts climbing to cross motorway, fork L (sp wasserwerk) and continue into woods. Pass waterworks L with motorway parallel R. At T-junction turn L, following waterworks fence L. Come out onto riverbank under motorway bridge and continue along flood dyke (Fleher Deich) past **Volmerswerth** R (42km) (accommodation, refreshments). Continue on Volmerswerth Deich across area of extensive market gardening (Appelkamp) and follow road as it curves R past sewerage works R. Pass under road bridge with Neuss visible across river L, then bear L along flood dyke and fork R (Auf den Steinen) into **Hamm** (46km) (refreshments).

Cross Fährstrasse into Hammer Dorfstrasse and after 50m fork L onto flood dyke (Am Sandacker) to return to riverbank just before modern railway bridge. For next 3.5km, route loops round between river L and Düsseldorf

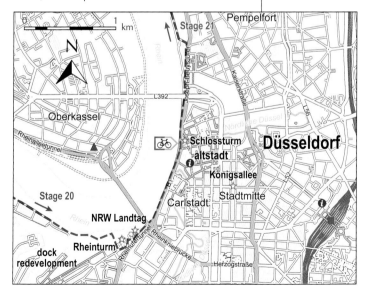

Schlossturm in the centre of Düsseldorf

harbour R. Pass power station R and golf course L. Emerge onto road (cycle track L) and where road bears R continue straight ahead continuing along flood dyke between river and harbour. ▶ Cross entrance to harbour via modern footbridge and continue on red cycle track. By old crane, just before **Rheinturm** tower, turn R away from river and L to circle clockwise to far side of tower. Bear L away from tower and pass modern Nordrhein-Westfalen **Landtag** (parliament) building L. Continue under Rheinkniebrücke and on along Mannesmannufer promenade (cycle lane L) to reach **Schlossturm** in centre of **Düsseldorf** (52km; 35m) (accommodation, refreshments, YH, tourist office, cycle shop, station).

The harbour has seen much redevelopment and has many interesting modern buildings.

Düsseldorf (pop. 590,000) is Germany's seventh-largest city and capital of Nordrhein-Westfalen. It first came to prominence in 1288 when the forces of Berg defeated those of Köln at the Battle of Worringen. In 1386, Düsseldorf became the capital of Berg, but its golden age was at the beginning of the 18th century under the rule of Kurfürst Jan Wellem. The city suffered in the aftermath of the Napoleonic Wars, when it became part of Prussia (1815). Prosperity returned with the Industrial

Düsseldorf town hall

Lake in middle of the 'Kö' (Königsallee), Düsseldorf

Revolution, and the population doubled between 1882 and 1892. The city was extensively bombed during the Second World War, but was rapidly rebuilt in the 1950s and 60s, the altstadt being restored as it was pre-war.

Modern Düsseldorf is an important commercial and financial centre, particularly renowned for fashion and media companies. The Messe exhibition hall complex is among the world's most important, holding nearly 20% of all premier trade shows. Competition with Köln remains strong, particularly with regard to sport and carnival, when Düsseldorfers drink copious quantities of a local beer called *alt*.

STAGE 21
Düsseldorf to Duisburg

Start	Schlossturm, Düsseldorf (35m)
Finish	Königstrasse, Duisburg (31m)
Distance	32km
Signposting	RR and D8 (both inconsistent) and local signage

After following the river closely through open country, the route encounters industrial suburbs after Serm. It circumnavigates two large steelworks using suburban streets and tracks before reaching the city of Duisburg, at the confluence of the Rhine and the Ruhr. The terrain is completely flat.

From riverside Schlossturm in **Düsseldorf** Altstadt continue N along the upper Rhine promenade (cycle lane R). Pass under Oberkasseler Brücke and continue past Musikverein concert hall R, Cenotaph war memorial L and Kunst Palast art gallery R. Bear L (Robert-Lehr-Ufer) and turn R on gravel track alongside Rheinpark R. Where gravel ends continue for 100m on asphalt and just before next bridge, turn R following track away from river for 100m. Turn L under bridge on cycle track beside Rotterdamer Strasse. Continue for 2.5km past **Düsseldorf Messe** exhibition centre (4km).

Just before last hall (Esprit Arena), continue ahead (sp wasserwerk) through car park and ahead on road parallel with river. At entrance to waterworks, continue on cycle track along flood dyke, following this for 5km, always on dyke apart from short section dropping down under road bridge. Where track meets road leading to Kaiserswerth–Langst-Kierst ferry, turn sharply L. Just before ferry, beside Alt Rheinfähre gasthaus, turn sharply R on to track that crosses bridge over sidestream then follows river past Kaiserpfalz Castle ruins and Suitbertus Abbey (both R) in **Kaiserswerth** (11.5km) (accommodation, refreshments).

Kaiserpfalz Castle (built in 1045) was located on the island of Werth. It became a temporary seat of the Holy Roman Emperor (Kaiser) and, to reflect this, in 1062 the island's name was changed to **Kaiserswerth** (pop. 7700). It was a collection point for Rhine tolls from 1174. Eventually the right branch of the river silted up, and Kaiserswerth ceased being an island. Its important strategic position on the river led to it being frequently fought over and it changed hands many times. Fortifications were demolished in 1702 and it became part of the Prussian Rhine province in 1815. Its monastic history (Suitbertus Abbey was founded around AD700) has led to a connection with medical care. Pioneering English nurse Florence Nightingale was trained in the Deaconess Clinic and during both world wars there were military hospitals here.

A British phone box in a suburban garden in Duisburg

Continue past Kaiserswerth altstadt, following river for 2.5km to beginning of Wittlaer. Turn sharply R (pedestrian path continues ahead) and after 100m L uphill

(Rheinuferweg becoming Zur Schwarzbachmündung). At end turn L (Schulweg) and continue on block track between hedges. At end bear L (Bockumer Strasse) and follow this road winding through **Wittlaer** (14km).

Continue for 1.5km, to reach bus turning circle at Lieversberg, just before end of village. Fork L onto quiet residential road (Rosspfad) and at end continue ahead between fields. Just before reaching flood dyke, bear R on asphalt country lane. Chimneys and blast furnaces of Duisburg are visible ahead. Turn L at crossing of lanes and after 500m, R at T-junction. After 400m turn R at T-junction and fork L after 200m. At next junction, by small white chapel L, turn R to reach **Serm** (19.5km) (accommodation, refreshments).

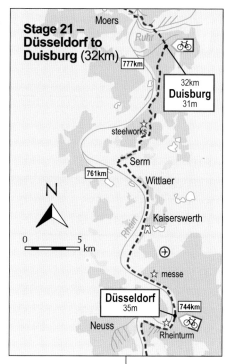

Continue through village for 1km on Dorfstrasse and turn L (Am Klapptor). Follow road R into Breitkamp and continue over main road (Krefelder Strasse). Turn immediately R (Am Heidberg), parallel with Krefelder Strasse and after 300m turn L into quiet lane. Turn R at next junction (Am Grünen Hang) and L after 250m onto gravel track between allotments L and woods R. Bear gently R at crossroads into Am Forkelsgraben, still between allotments and woods, past sports club L and cross next road. Turn immediately L on gravel cycle track in trees between main road L and Angerbach stream R. Dog-leg R and L across Mündelheimerstrasse, continuing on gravel track parallel with stream. Turn R across stream and R on other side to join a track contouring around side of landscaped ex-slagheap. Bear R on short cobbled track and cross road into Goetzkestrasse. Bear R at T-junction (Steinbrinkstrasse) and continue to reach staggered main road junction in Angerhausen.

Bear ahead L on cycle track beside Kaiserswerther-strasse. Turn L at traffic lights (Molberg Strasse), and where this bears R, turn L (Am Kreuzaker) and imme-diately R (Am Tollberg). At end, cross Ehringer Strasse and tram tracks, continuing ahead into Friemersheimer Strasse. Follow this road, bearing R (Augsburgerstrasse becoming Wittlaererstrasse) with riverbank behind houses L. Continue along Rheinuferweg, and where road bears away R, continue ahead into riverside park passing canoe club R and house R with red British phone box in garden. At end of park, bear R to reach mostly cobbled Wanheimer Strasse. Turn L (cycle lane on both sides), continue over level crossing and emerge onto main road.

Turn L (still called Wanheimer Strasse) along cycle track L of road, and immediately cross to R at first crossing. Continue N for 2km, dog-legging R and L to go over rail-way bridge. Immediately before Marienhospital tram sta-tion, cross tram tracks and fork L alongside Wörthstrasse.

Duisburg, with the state theatre and opera house (left) and new city palace (right)

Just before road bends R, where there is a sign commemorating pioneers of Duisburg including August Thyssen, turn R on small alley through old wall. Emerge onto residential Hochfeldstrasse and continue through area of old industrial housing. Bear R at Brückenplatz and immediately L to follow Heerstrasse (busy road, no cycle lane!) for 750m. Bear R under flyover into Steinsche Gasse (cycle track R). This leads to junction with pedestrianised Königstrasse R in centre of **Duisburg** (32km; 31m) (accommodation, refreshments, YH, tourist office, cycle shop, station).

Duisburg's position at the confluence of the Rhine and the Ruhr has made it an important trading city. Although it was a Hanseatic League city in the 14th century, the 19th-century Industrial Revolution was the catalyst for manufacturing growth and prosperity. Duisburg became the world's largest inland

Modern sculpture in Königstrasse, Duisburg

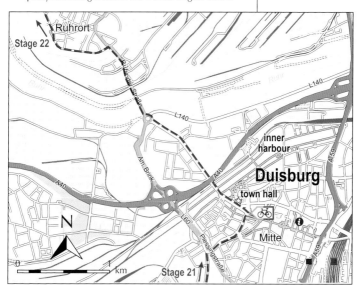

197

Duisburg, with the town hall tower (left) and Salvator church (right)

port and one of Germany's major production centres for iron and steel, dominated by the giant Krupp and Thyssen companies. Today, it accounts for 50% of German steel output. Because of its key role in German industry and transportation, Duisburg was one of the most heavily bombed cities of the Second World War, with 299 raids destroying 80% of the city. Post-war reconstruction has replaced this destruction, but nevertheless Duisburg remains an industrial city. A great influx of immigrant labour, mostly Turks, has created a cosmopolitan environment and Duisburg is home to the largest mosque outside Muslim countries.

STAGE 22
Duisburg to Xanten

Start	Königstrasse, Duisburg (31m)
Finish	Xanten main square (29m)
Distance	51km
Signposting	RR and D8 (both inconsistent) and local signage

Gradually leaving the industrialised region behind, the Rhine meanders widely across extensive agricultural flood plains. This is true big-sky country with seemingly endless horizons. The area was badly affected by floods in 1995, and much work has been undertaken to raise flood dykes and create new relief polders. Much of the route is on good tracks along or beside these dykes.

From junction of Steinsche Gasse and Königstrasse in **Duisburg** centre, take Schwanenstrasse heading NW with cycle lane R, passing town hall and Salvator church (both R). Cross Schwanentor Brücke lifting bridge over inner harbour, pass under motorway and continue on Ruhrorter Strasse, to reach roundabout. Take second exit from roundabout, switching over to cycle track L, and cross three bridges over Ruhr and branches of Duisburg harbour. Immediately after third bridge, turn L (Krausstrasse) and follow riverbank bending R. Where promenade drops towards old paddle steamer (museum ship), bear R away from river (Dammstrasse) to pass Schifferbörse L. This attractive street is lined by old shipping company offices in area called **Ruhrort** (3km) (accommodation, refreshments).

At end of buildings, fork R and follow cycle lane L of road up onto Rhine bridge. Cross river using cycle track L. At end of bridge take second turning L (Ruhrorter Strasse), and after 100m cross road to turn sharply R back under bridge (Dammstrasse). Bear R beside little-used harbour and turn L on lifting bridge over harbour mouth. Continue ahead on gravel track with fields R. After 1km,

Paddle steamer museum ship at Ruhrort

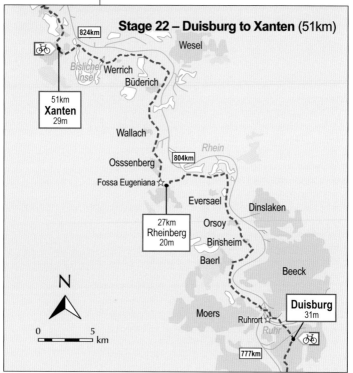

Stage 22 – Duisburg to Xanten (51km)

824km

Wesel

Bislicher Insel

Werrich

Büderich

51km
Xanten
29m

Wallach

Rhein

804km

Osssenberg

Fossa Eugeniana ☆

Eversael

Dinslaken

27km
Rheinberg
20m

Orsoy

Binsheim

Baerl

Beeck

N

0   5
km

Moers

Ruhrort ☆

Duisburg
31m

Ruhr

777km

bear R to pick up flood dyke and cycle along this (becoming asphalt) bearing L. Where dyke comes close to road, drop down R onto gravel track running below dyke beside river for 1.2km. Rejoin dyke and follow asphalt road under railway and motorway bridges. Continue beneath avenue of lime trees past Haus Rheinblick (refreshments). Continue on gravel track to reach next junction, turning L on asphalt track through fields to enter **Baerl** (refreshments) on Hofstrasse (10.5km).

At beginning of village turn R (Steinschenstrasse) and fork L (Paschmannstrasse). After 300m, fork R (Dammstrasse) and bear L onto flood dyke. Bear L at junction and drop L to follow red block track below dyke. Climb back onto dyke at road junction then follow this country lane (Woltershofer Strasse) L away from dyke to join main road (Orsoyer Strasse) and reach **Binsheim** (14km).

Cycle route uses country lanes to bypass village. Turn L (Sardmannsbruchweg), then turn R through fields. Turn R at T-junction and turn L on cycle track alongside main road to reach **Orsoy** (16km) (accommodation, refreshments, cycle shop).

> **Orsoy** was a heavily fortified town with walls built in three stages between 1273 and 1640, of which some ruins and one tower (the Pulverturm) remain. For 90 years from 1851 the town's principal industry was cigar production. This ceased during the Second World War, when raw materials became unobtainable.

Continue ahead through village. After railway level crossing, cycle track commences L, following road curving round large coal harbour behind dyke R. After 1km, turn R onto block track and follow this for 7km, always parallel with and below dyke R. En route pass wildfowl reserve between dyke and **Eversael** L. At Milchplatz, ignore both road branching L towards farm and the track up onto dyke. Just after Milchplatz, follow dyke as it turns sharply L. ▶

N of Milchplatz, gravel extraction work has cut the original course of the flood dyke. A new dyke, which the route follows, has been constructed passing S of this area.

To visit Rheinberg (pop. 32,000) (accommodation, refreshments, tourist office, cycle shop, station) continue ahead across bypass and follow cycle track alongside Fossa Eugeniana canal into town. Regain route by leaving NW on Xantener Strasse.

Continue alongside dyke, crossing series of tracks coming up from L, to reach barrier where rough asphalt road bears R through gap in dyke. Follow this and after 250m turn L on asphalt road away from dyke with Rheinberg visible ahead. Follow road curving gently R, then turn L to reach busy **Rheinberg** bypass (27km, 20m). ◄

Turn R on cycle track R of road and continue past traffic lights at junction with Xantener Strasse. Just before filling station L, fork R away from road parallel with railway (Werftstrasse). Turn R over level crossing and bear L following railway with Solvay chemical works L and **Fossa Eugeniana** canal behind railway R. Pass **Ossenberg** L (29.5km).

Fossa Eugeniana canal is a 50km-long, 4.3m-wide canal connecting the Rhine and Meuse, and is named after Princess Eugenia, daughter of the Spanish King Phillip II. Construction started in 1626 but was never completed. The canal was built by the Spanish to provide an alternative route from Germany to the North Sea bypassing the Netherlands, and thus cut off Spain's rebellious Dutch provinces from profitable Rhine trade. It was also intended to form a protective ditch against Dutch incursion, for which it was lined with 24 bastions. Today the canal is derelict, although towpaths have been opened up for walkers and cyclists.

The old Fossa Eugeniana canal, Rheinberg

Bear L away from railway and turn immediately R (An der Momm). Bear L through barrier to follow cycle track running below crest of flood dyke. Just before track drops down L onto road, fork R onto asphalt track along top of dyke. Bear R through barrier and continue across railway line following top of dyke for 6km. Bear L, passing bar L and dog-leg across road junction. Dyke winds along beside new flood relief polder at Niederwallach R, then continues past **Büderich** (36.5km) (accommodation, refreshments).

New road bridge at Wesel

Pass Wacht am Rhein hotel L, where dyke comes close to river R, and continue along dyke for 2km. Approaching new Rhine bridge at Wesel, bear L off dyke and R parallel with old road. Turn L to dog-leg across old road and continue ahead passing under new bridge road on yellow block track. Continue ahead forking R of dyke, track becoming gravel and bear L to dog-leg over disused railway.

At 1.95km long, **Wesel railway bridge** (built in 1874) was the longest in Germany until the Hindenburgbrücke opened near Rüdesheim in 1913 (see Stage 16). Widened in 1927, it was destroyed by the retreating German army in March 1945.

Entrance to St Victor's Cathedral, Xanten

Route circles old fort in trees L, then continues just below crest of dyke R, passing TV mast, series of farms and large new gravel works (all L). Drop down off dyke L and turn R onto road which bears round in front of houses L below dyke. At end of houses, continue ahead just below crest of dyke and follow this to reach road near **Werrich** (43.5km). Turn R on quiet country road (Eylander Weg) winding across **Bislicher Insel** (46.5km).

> **Bislicher Insel** is a large area of low-lying land in the bend of an old Rhine course now used as winter flood relief polder and waterfowl sanctuary. Over 25,000 geese overwinter here, and many other species, including Redshanks, can be seen.

Pass visitors centre R (refreshments) and continue to reach riverbank. Cross bridge over sidestream (Alte Rhein) to reach road leading to Xanten–Marwick ferry (refreshments), and turn L (Gelderner Strasse). Continue ahead, passing through flood dyke and cross main road at traffic lights. Climb uphill on cycle track beside road R, and turn R (Viktorstrasse). Follow this into partly cobbled Marsstrasse, to reach Marktplatz in centre of **Xanten** (51km; 29m) (accommodation, refreshments, YH, camping, tourist office, cycle shop, station).

> **Xanten** (pop. 21,500) – the only German town name that starts with an X – is the site of Ulpia Traiana, the second-largest town in Roman Germania (after Köln) and home to the 30th Legion. As such it was heavily fortified and had important civil buildings, including an amphitheatre. In AD363 Viktor of Xanten was martyred here, and St Viktor's Cathedral (started 982, completed 1263) was later built over his burial place. Of the medieval fortifications, the best preserved part is Kleve Gate, while the Roman city has been opened up as an archaeological park.

STAGE 23
Xanten to Arnhem

Start	Xanten main square (29m)
Finish	Arnhem station (23m)
Distance	67km
Signposting	RR (inconsistent) Xanten–Millingen, LF3b Millingen–Arnhem

More big-sky country as the Rhine continues to meander across a broad agricultural flood plain with scattered communities. The river enters the Netherlands at Millingen an der Rijn, where it starts dividing into various channels flowing onwards towards the North Sea. Much use is again made of flood dykes. Once in the Netherlands, the river is crossed twice by ferry.

From NW corner of Marktplatz (**Xanten**'s main square), turn L (Karthaus) and continue, forking R into Rheinstrasse. Dropping down out of town, go ahead at roundabout with broken arch in centre and continue on cycle track R passing archaeological park with Roman **amphitheatre** L. Cross main road and continue on cycle track R of Salmstrasse into **Luttingen** (1.5km).

Dog-leg R and L (still Salmstrasse), bearing L at end (Fischerstrasse). Continue through village and at end go ahead through gap in fence and turn R onto gravel track along shore of Xantaner **Südsee** lake. After 500m, turn R through another fence gap and L along road. At beginning of village, turn L (Am Bossacker), then R (Am Dickend) and L again (Am Eickacker). At end turn R into Scholtenstrasse and continue past **Wardt** L (4.5km).

At end, turn sharply L away from flood dyke (still Scholtenstrasse). Bear R then dog-leg L. Just before T-junction, fork R onto cycle track through trees on opposite side of stream from road. Pass holiday house estate R and continue ahead through car park to reach Xantener **Nordsee**. Turn R along lakeshore on red block track,

becoming gravel as it bears L around lake for 2km. Where track divides, fork R, and at second fork, fork L. At end of lake, turn R (sp Obermörmter) and follow track up onto flood dyke. Bear L following asphalt track winding along top of dyke (Rheindamm) for 2.5km, passing Vynen sailing club and houses below dyke L. Drop down L off dyke (Hoher Weg) into **Obermörmter** (10.5km).

Vynen church, seen across Xantener Nordsee

Turn R at crossroads and where main road bears L, keep straight on (Papenweg) along cycle lane L, with spire of St Petrus church visible ahead. Where road turns L at beginning of **Scholtenhof**, go straight ahead and turn R on red block track up onto flood dyke. When dyke forks, take R (older, lower) dyke alongside Rhine and follow this bearing L past Husen caravan park R and campsite L (refreshments, camping). Bend R and L past farm on track, which becomes gravel. Turn L at Rees ferry road (wide but little used since opening of bridge) and follow this, crossing flood dyke, into **Niedermörmter** (15km).

Turn R at T-junction (Rheinstrasse) with cycle track R and continue through village. At end of village pass under bridge road, and after 250m turn R (Goetendyk), and R again past farms. Just before reaching bridge, turn L through gate and L again on red block track alongside flood dyke. Follow this for 1.5km, then where road comes

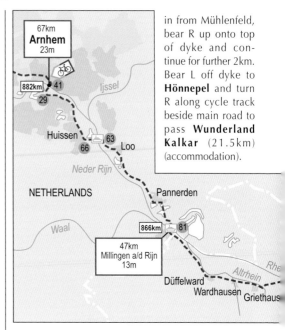

in from Mühlenfeld, bear R up onto top of dyke and continue for further 2km. Bear L off dyke to **Hönnepel** and turn R along cycle track beside main road to pass **Wunderland Kalkar** (21.5km) (accommodation).

Block paving, typical of tracks along the flood dykes of the Niederrhein

Wunderland Kalkar theme park is constructed inside the buildings of a nuclear power station that was never opened. Construction started in 1972 on what was intended to be Germany's first plutonium-fuelled fast breeder reactor. Completed in 1985, it cost $4billion. Following the Chernobyl disaster in 1986, it never went into production and the project was cancelled in 1991. From afar, the most noticeable of 40 attractions is a large swing ride that emerges from the top of the cooling tower. Kalkar attracts over 600,000 visitors annually, many of them Dutch.

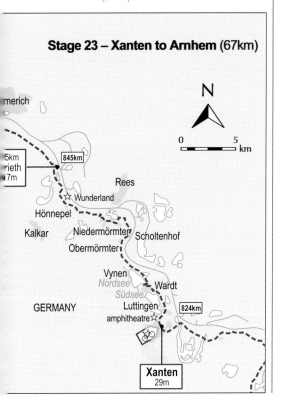

Stage 23 – Xanten to Arnhem (67km)

N

0 — 5 km

merich

5km
rieth
7m

845km

Rees

☆ Wunderland

Hönnepel

Kalkar   Niedermörmter   Scholtenhof
          Obermörmter

Vynen
Nordsee   ●—Wardt
Südsee

GERMANY   Luttingen   824km
           amphitheatre ☆

🚲

Xanten
29m

Turn R at roundabout, initially on cycle lane beside road, then on road bearing L along flood dyke to reach **Grieth** (25km; 17m) (accommodation, refreshments).

Fork R into village (Schuldamm) and turn R onto dyke (Schifferdamm) with fishermen's cottages below dyke L. Bear L, pass church and turn L to reach Marktplatz. Continue on Schlossstrasse and leave village bearing L to T-junction by windmill. Turn R (Rheinuferstrasse) on cycle track beside road L, and continue along flood dyke for 7km with Emmerich visible across river R. Dog-leg L and R to cross Emmerich Bridge approach road at traffic lights. ◀ Continue on flood dyke for further 3.5km to reach small bridge over Alt Rhein. Immediately after this bridge, turn R onto asphalt track along dyke beside old river. Pass over new sluice with **Griethausen** below dyke L (37km).

Emmerich Bridge is the longest suspension bridge in Germany.

The preserved **iron bridge** running north from Griethausen across Alt Rhein is part of the infrastructure from the first Rhine railway crossing. Opened in 1865, the Kleve to Emmerich line crossed the Rhine by train ferry between Spyck and Welle after the Prussian government had objected to a fixed bridge for military reasons. The train ferry ceased operation in 1926, although the line remained in use serving Spyck mill until 1987.

From ④ continue along dyke (Am alten Rhein), with Kleve (YH) visible L, to reach sluice and locks at **Wardhausen** (39km) (refreshments). Turn R (Johanna-Sebus-Strasse) and branch R along top of flood dyke. ◀ Follow this for 8km, passing above **Düffelward** (41km), Keeken and Binnen to cross unmarked German–Dutch border and arrive directly at **Millingen an der Rijn** ferry (47km; 13m) (accommodation, refreshments, camping, tourist office, cycle shop).

Signposted route from Wardhausen to Millingen a/d Rijn stays on road through Düffelward ⑤, Keeken and Bimmen. Although route along dyke is marked 'private', it is open for permissive use by walkers and cyclists.

Cross Rhine by pedestrian ferry and turn L ⑧¹ on concrete track along dyke [sp LF3b]. Cross sluice for Oude Waal and turn sharply L past brickworks R. Turn R, passing another brickworks L and continue on

German–Dutch border at the entrance to Millingen an der Rijn

Lobberdenseweg between two worked-out gravel pits. Cross road on top of flood dyke and continue ahead, bearing L (Haspelstraat) into **Pannerden** (50.5km) (refreshments).

Turn L at T-junction (Schoolstraat) and bear L at square into Kerkstraat, passing church R. Climb up onto dyke and turn R (Rijndijk). Ahead at crossroads 88 on road along dyke for 4km, crossing Kandia sluice. Pass red stone elephant statue R near portal of new Neder Rijn rail tunnel. Turn L at T-junction, continuing along dyke to reach crossroads 65. Continue on dyke, bearing L to pass **Loo** R (56km).

Continue past village to road junction 64 and continue along dyke, now on quiet road. At fork 63, bear L (Looveerweg) dropping down from dyke to reach ferry terminal. Cross Neder Rijn by car ferry and continue ahead on cycle track beside road L. At main road (Stadsdam), turn R (staying on L of road) and after 50m turn L into **Huissen** 66 (60km; 13m) (refreshments).

Turn first R (Langestraat) through centre of town. Just before this drops into underpass, bear R and turn immediately L. At T-junction, turn R, crossing main road beside roundabout and continue N on cycle track along dyke parallel with main road L. Continue past roundabout and point **30**. Pass under motorway bridge and immediately turn R up to higher level. At top, turn L and fork R along flood dyke for 3.5km, curving L with water meadows and river R, to reach point **22** just before first road bridge. Fork R to continue under bridge and join slip road leading to second bridge. At T-junction **29**, turn R parallel with main road onto bridge over water meadows. After 300m cross slip road, and dog-leg L and R onto red asphalt cycle track parallel with main road. Cross Neder Rijn to reach Willemsplein **41** in front of **Arnhem** station (67km; 23m) (accommodation, refreshments, YH, tourist office, cycle shop, station).

When **Arnhem** (pop. 146,000) was first established in 1233 it was beside a small hill some distance from the Rhine; in 1530, however, the river changed course to flow past the city. Arnhem is unusual for the Netherlands, in that half of its suburbs (to the north and west) are hilly.

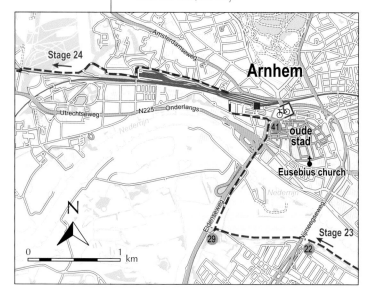

STAGE 24
Arnhem to Wijk bij Duurstede

Start	Arnhem station (23m)
Finish	Dijkstraat, Wijk bij Duurstede (7m)
Distance	51km
Signposting	LF4b (Arnhem–Amerongen)

Arnhem sits at the beginning of a low, sandy ridge that extends north-west, and until it reaches Amerongen the route undulates between the forested slopes of this ridge and water meadows beside the Neder Rijn. Turning away from the hills, the river dyke is followed across flat polder land to Wijk bij Duurstede.

From Willemsplein in front of **Arnhem** station ④①, head W on cycle track alongside Utrechtsestraat. Pass bus station and turn R (Brugstraat). Cross railway bridge and turn L (Noordelijke Parallelweg) alongside railway L. After 900m, fork L and bear L around railway yards. Turn R

Bridge at Arnhem, with scaffolding-covered cathedral (left)

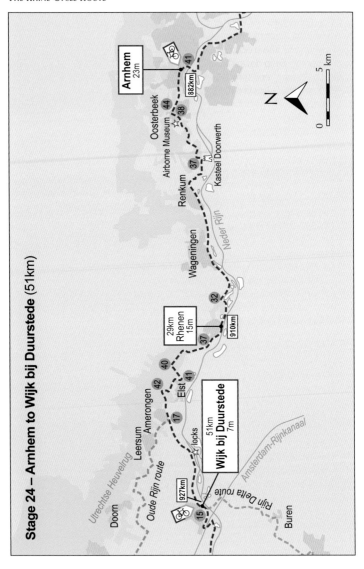

Stage 24 – Arnhem to Wijk bij Duurstede (51km)

at traffic lights into Heijenoordseweg (one-way street) using multi-use path L. Bear R and turn immediately L on cycle lane into trees (Diependalseweg) with primary school R. Drop down through woods of Landgoed Mariendaal and at end turn L under bridge and immediately R uphill (Driegemeentenpad) parallel to railway R. Continue ahead uphill over crossroads on cycle track parallel to railway R. Continue into Parallelweg and turn L at crossroads ⓸ into Stationsweg on red cycle lane R. Cross main road (Utrechtseweg) and after 75m turn R ㉖ on easily missed cycle track into Park Hartenstein to pass **Airborne Museum** (visible through trees R) at **Oosterbeeck** (5.5km) (refreshments).

The **Airborne Museum** in Hartenstein House recalls the events of September 1944 when Arnhem was the scene of the largest airborne assault of the Second World War. As Allied armies advanced across northwest Europe in autumn 1944, it became clear that an all-out assault upon Germany would be greatly aided if bridgeheads could be secured over the Rhine. To this end, airborne troops were dropped behind enemy lines on 17 September, tasked with seizing and holding the bridges at Nijmegen and Arnhem for two days until relieved by the advancing main army.

The result was heroic but tragic. While the north side of Arnhem Bridge was initially secured, poor weather and greater-than-expected numbers of enemy troops held up the main advance. Allied troops were forced to retreat to a position around Oosterbeeck, which they held for several days before retreating by boat across the Rhine to the safety of the arriving main force after nine days of action. Of almost 10,600 troops dropped, 2398 escaped, 1485 died and 6714 were captured. Arnhem Bridge was not finally captured until 14 April 1945. A book, and the 1977 film of the action, was poignantly titled *A Bridge too Far*.

Follow asphalt cycle track winding downhill through trees and occasional fields. Turn sharply R over small valley, and sharply L to continue alongside pond L. Bear L onto road for short distance and immediately turn R opposite cottage. Pass paddocks and stables of riding school R, and bear L through woods. Just before reaching next road, turn R uphill, still through woods and fields. Bear L downhill and turn L at T-junction onto red block track. Emerge through gate onto road, bearing L to reach roundabout. Turn R and after 50m turn L (Bentincklaan). Fork immediately L (Italiaanseweg), continuing through woods with large houses set among trees. Cross next road, going straight over to continue through woods. After 300m, turn R opposite white house and continue to reach end of Spechtlaan. Do not go into Spechtlaan, rather turn L and then fork L to reach Holleweg and drop steeply down through woods to reach main road **37**. Turn R and pass entrance to **Kasteel Doorwerth** castle L (11km) (refreshments).

Drawbridge at Doorwerth Castle

216

The first castle at **Doorwerth** was built around 1260, but its present appearance dates back to 1560. Originally surrounded only by a moat, the dyke was added in 1637 to protect the castle from Rhine floods. The castle fell into disrepair, but was restored in the early 20th century. Heavily damaged by shelling in 1944, it was again restored and is now a museum run by a local foundation.

Continue along road in edge of woods. After 550m, where road turns R uphill, continue ahead on broad cycle track to reach approach road to motorway bridge over Neder Rijn. Turn L, then R under motorway and R again climbing up to road. Dog-leg R and L to continue alongside motorway. Follow track as it bears away from motorway to go under road bridge. Continue past Heelsum church R on Koninginnelaan, and fork L (Kerkweg), dropping down and up again into Heelsum (refreshments, cycle shop). Turn L at main road (Utrechtseweg) and follow this on cycle lane R downhill past **Renkum** L (15km) (accommodation, refreshments, cycle shop).

At bottom of hill, where Utrechtseweg ends, follow cycle lane round L and cross Renkum bypass (Rijksweg). Bear R on cycle lane L of this road for 1.7km passing paper mills L and continuing into open country. Where main road starts ascending, turn L and follow quiet country lane alongside hill, with water meadows L. Join road coming from Randwijk ferry, following this gently uphill for 200m and fork L ⑧¹ onto Veerweg. After 800m, turn L winding along flood dyke (Grebbdijk) with water meadows L and **Wageningen** R (20km) (accommodation, refreshments).

Join road at T-junction and bear L passing harbour for Rheinvallei mills L. Continue to reach marina and fork L along dyke on quiet road with cycle lane. Continue for 2km to ㉔ then further 1km to reach main road. Turn L on cycle track for 75m ㉜ and L again on cycle track (Cuneralaan) parallel with canal. Continue alongside Neder Rijn for 2.5km to pass under Rhenen Bridge ㊱. Bear L, dropping down off dyke across water meadows beside river, with view of Cunera church and old wind-mill in **Rhenen** R (29km; 15m) (accommodation, refreshments, station).

Between Remmerden and Amerongen route follows LF4b winding through attractive wooded hills of Utrechtse Heuvelrug National Park. This can be avoided by remaining on main road through Elst.

Continue on road (Rijnkade), turning R (Veerweg) away from river opposite riverside restaurant. At main road (Utrechtsestraatweg), turn L along cycle track R past 36 and continue ahead at roundabout for 1.5km to beginning of Remmerden 37. Turn R beside farm (Stokweg) and wind uphill to T-junction. ◀ Turn L, then R and L again in front of gates to large house. Where Stokweg turns R, continue ahead between fields to reach Utrechtse Heuvelrug forest. Follow asphalt cycle track (Defensieweg) winding through forest for 3km, crossing number of dirt tracks, but always staying on asphalt to reach road 40. Turn L downhill (Veenendaalsestraatweg) to reach edge of **Elst** (36km).

Turn R on cobbled residential street (Franseweg), and first R 41 (Driftweg) uphill back towards forest. At beginning of trees, turn L on asphalt cycle track and follow this winding through forest for 2km to 42. Turn sharply L, and descend through forest mostly on asphalt but some short sections of gravel. Emerge from forest bearing R past sports club L, then L on gravel track to reach main road. Turn R (Koningin Wilhelminaweg) to reach **Amerongen** (41km) (accommodation, refreshments).

Huge sluice gates, like these near Amerongen, control river flow

*The world's only
drive-through
windmill at Wijk bij
Duurstede*

At outskirts of village, turn L (Burg Jhr H v d Boschstraat) and L again (Holleweg). Bear R at T-junction past church R, and continue into Drostestraat. Pass entrance to Amerongen Castle L and reach ⑰. ▶ Continue out of village on Lekdijk and follow this country road along flood dyke for 8.5km, passing ⑯ and further on Amerongen **locks** and huge semi-circular sluices L (45.5km). Road becomes Rijndijk and crosses small bridge over Kromme Rijn. Bear L, then fork R (Bemmelsdijk), passing under world's only drive-through windmill in **Wijk bij Duurstede** (51km; 7m) (accommodation, refreshments, tourist office cycle shop).

At this point we leave LF4b, which turns R (Donkerstraat) and marks the beginning of the Oude Rijn alternative route.

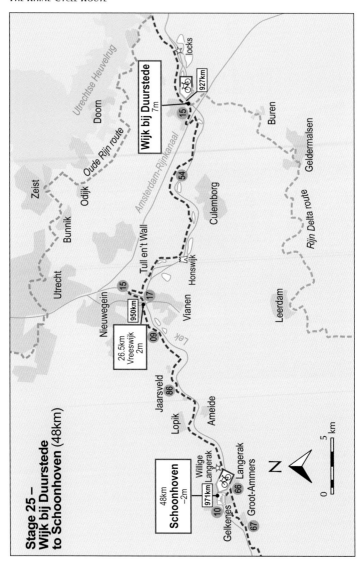

Stage 25 –
Wijk bij Duurstede
to Schoonhoven (48km)

STAGE 25
Wijk bij Duurstede to Schoonhoven

Start	Dijkstraat, Wijk bij Duurstede (7m)
Finish	Schoonhoven ferry (−2m)
Distance	48km
Signposting	local

The Rhine divides again, with the Amsterdam–Rijn Kanaal and narrow winding Oude Rijn both branching off north-west. The countryside is flat cultivated polder land, mostly below sea level, protected by high flood dykes and sluice gates. The whole of this stage is on quiet country roads along the top of the dyke on the north side of the widely meandering Lek, the Rhine arm that reaches the North Sea at Hoek van Holland. From the dyke you look down on fertile, farming countryside, with a string of prosperous farms alongside. Extensive orchards around Wijk give way to cattle in fields, sheep along dykes, geese on lakes and goats or horses in paddocks.

Leave **Wijk bij Duurstede** on Dijkstraat. Cross flood dyke and follow cycle track below dyke to reach ramp for Wijk–Riswijk car ferry L **15**. ▶ Cross ramp and continue along Lekdijk Oost, dropping down R below dyke for short distance before climbing back onto dyke. Bear L to pass houses at Wijk sluice L, with locks at entrance to Amsterdam Rijnkanaal behind. Turn L on cycle track beside main road to cross locks, then turn immediately L along dyke (Lekdijk West). Bear R after 700m and follow flood dyke for 2km to rejoin road. Continue on top of flood dyke for 18km as it winds along on N side of River Lek. Pass **96** with Beusichen ferry L, **54** where route bears L onto quiet road, and **52** by turn for Culemborg ferry, with Culemborg visible across river. Drop down briefly to pass under railway bridge, and at **51** pass a line of 20th-century concrete blockhouses and fortifications running through fields. Pass Honswijk–Everdingen passenger ferry and circle round moated **Honswijk Castle**

The Rijn Delta alternative route uses ferry to cross river, following LF17.

221

Recently rethatched
Dutch farmhouse
below Lekdijk

L (17km), one of a chain of fortifications known as Dutch waterline forts.

During the wars of independence from Spain (1568–1648), the Dutch realised the value of using flood waters to defend against enemy invasion. In 1629 a programme commenced of building sluices and dykes to enable flooding of low-lying land in case of attack. These were protected by a line of fortresses running from north to south, crossing the Lek at Schoonhoven. After the creation of the Netherland Kingdom in 1815, a new **waterline defence system** was constructed further east, crossing the Lek at Honswijk between Culemborg and Vreeswijk. This was activated in 1870 during the Franco-Prussian war, but never attacked.

Continue past ⑱ at turn for Hagestein locks and sluices L, and pass above village of **Tull en't Wall** R (21km) (camping), with views of tall buildings in Utrecht on horizon. Dog-leg R under motorway bridge and turn

R alongside Lekkanaal to (16). Just before Prinses Beatrix locks, turn L off road (15) and bear R to pass lock houses L. Turn L at end of locks to cross over canal and turn immediately L (Voorhavendijk) along opposite side. Continue along dyke, bearing R by mouth of canal and passing fort R to reach **Vreeswijk** (26.5km; 2m) (accommodation, refreshments).

Passing through **Vreeswijk** is like a history lesson in canal building. The route crosses four sets of locks (*sluis*), dating from the 14th to the 20th centuries, all built to provide canal connections between Utrecht and the Rhine. The oldest, Spuisluis, dates from 1373 and is Europe's oldest pound lock (two sets of gates with a chamber between). The picturesque Oudesluis (1818), with lifting bridges both ends and surrounded by pretty houses, is in the middle of the village, while Konigsluis (1892) is west of the centre and modern Prinses Beatrixsluis (1938), capable of taking ocean-going vessels, is east of the village.

In Vreeswijk, Spuisluis is the world's oldest pound lock, dating from 1373

Jaarsveld, monument to a Halifax bomber that crashed in 1943 with two survivors

Pass Spuisluis R and soon reach lifting bridge over canal at Oudesluis. Cross canal past ⑰, and continue on Molenstraat past church L then bear R to reach Koningsluis. Bear L over canal to ⑲, then immediately L and R along Lekboulevard passing turn for Neuwegein–Vianen ferry ⑳ and marina R. Pass ㉕ and at approach to motorway, take middle fork of three, dropping down to pass under bridge. Continue out of village on winding road along flood dyke for 19km, passing successively ⑨, holiday home complex at Klein Scheveningen L (refreshments, camping), and **Uitweg** (34km) below R. Just before pretty village of **Jaarsveld** ㊏ (37km) there is glass case R containing engine from Halifax bomber that crashed (1943) with two survivors. Continue past Jaarsfeld–Ameide ferry L ⑭, campsite at Salmsteke L and junction for Lopik ㊑. Before **Willige Langerak** (45.5km) route passes houses and farms R where colony of storks has occupied every tall nesting point. Opposite

Schoonhoven marina L, cycle track drops down off dyke R (sp Schoonhoven) to pass under main road and continue to centre of **Schoonhoven** (48km; –2m) (accommodation, refreshments, tourist office, cycle shop). ▶

Schoonhoven (pop. 12,000) is an old medieval town originally protected by city walls. These were extended in the early 17th century as part of the Dutch waterline fortifications, but were mostly removed in 1816 when a new waterline system was created further east. One city gate, Veerport, remains and has been incorporated within the flood defence system. Traditional industries include shipbuilding, silversmithing and clockmaking. There is a silver museum and silversmith's school, while the town hall clock and carillon is a fine example of local clockmaking. The centre of town is based along the attractive old canal, Oude Haven.

To bypass Schoonhoven, continue on dyke to main road, turning L along cycle track L to reach Schoonhoven–Gelkenes ferry **10**.

Veerpoort is the last remaining city gate in Schoonhoven

STAGE 26
Schoonhoven to Rotterdam

Start	Schoonhoven ferry (−2m)
Finish	Erasmus Bridge, Rotterdam (1m)
Distance	37km
Signposting	Local then LF11b from Kinderdijk to Rotterdam

The route continues across low-lying Dutch polder land, now south of the Lek, partly along flood dykes, with the surrounding countryside below sea level. At Kinderdijk, the route passes the finest collection of preserved windmills in the Netherlands. This stage ends in the sprawling industrial city of Rotterdam, where dedicated cycle tracks enable cyclists to reach the city centre with no significant on-road cycling.

Leave **Schoonhoven** by taking ferry to **Gelkenes**. Bear L (Versedijk) at top of ramp, then fork R along cycle lane below dyke L. Climb up onto dyke and turn sharply R at 66 into Tienweg, dropping down again. Cross main road and continue ahead on cycle lane L, with industrial area R. At T-junction, turn R (Haarsteeg) and R again (Liesveld), following round L grounds of moated house on site of old fort, to reach flood dyke and turn L onto cycle lane on road along dyke (Voorstraat). Approaching **Groot-Ammers**, follow road bearing L off dyke to wind through village and reach 67 (5.5km).

Bear R, and at end of village road climbs back onto dyke and continues for 2.5km to 06. Turn L, and after 300m R onto gravel cycle track alongside drainage ditch between fields. Pass **Eendenkooi Nature Reserve** R (8.5km), with basket nesting boxes for ducks suspended over watercourse. Turn R (Halfweg), heading back towards river and rejoin road along flood dyke. Turn L and continue past beautifully restored windmill (De Liefde) R and marina R to reach **Streefkerk** (12.5km) (refreshments).

Continue through village and after 1km turn L into easily missed Zudeweg, quiet country road without cycle lane. At crossroads **05** continue ahead on asphalt cycle track alongside drainage canal. Dog-leg around pond and cross bigger canal by humpback bridge. Turn sharply

Duck nesting baskets at Eendenkooi Nature Reserve

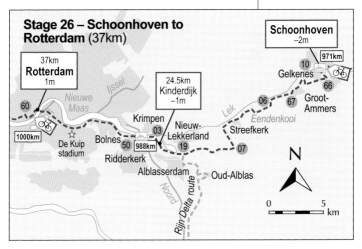

227

R 07 and continue on winding cycle track parallel to navigable canal R (hidden by high reeds in summer) for 3km to reach 19 (21km). Here route is joined by Rijn Delta alternative route (LF11), which has reached here from Wijk bij Duurstede by circuitous route via Linge river and Biesbosch marshes. Continue ahead over little canal bridge along cycle track with canals on both sides. After 600m bear R, where you are confronted with one of the Netherlands' most iconic sights, an avenue of 19 windmills, mostly in excellent state of repair with some of them working. Continue between windmills for 2.5km, bearing R at 02 to reach modern pumping station and visitor centre at **Kinderdijk** 03 (24.5km; −1m) (accommodation, refreshments).

Kinderdijk has the greatest concentration of windmills in the Netherlands

The Ablasserwaard polders between the Lek and Noord rivers were drained in the 13th century. However, as the land dried out it sank, while river levels rose due to silting up of the riverbed. By the 18th century a new system of drainage was needed and a system of 19 windmills was constructed at **Kinderdijk**. The mills are of two main designs – eight brick (built in 1738) and eight thatched (1740)

– plus two stone (1760) and a much older windmill from 1521 that was incorporated into the scheme.

In 1869, the windmills were replaced by a steam pumping station, itself superseded by diesel power in 1927. During the Second World War, a shortage of diesel oil led to the windmills being pressed back into service. A new, more powerful diesel pumping station was opened in the 1970s and capacity was doubled by adding an electric station in 1981. The Kinderdijk windmills have been UNESCO heritage listed since 1997 and many have been restored to working order.

Turn L (Molenstraat) on cycle track along top of dyke R. After 100m, fork R following dyke, then turn L behind houses. At end turn R to reach ferry terminal. Take passenger ferry on R. This sails to **Ridderkerk** on S side of Nieuwe Maas, via a stop in **Krimpen** (weekdays all year, last dep. 1725; weekends May–September only, last dep. 1710). ▸

Ferry on L is vehicle ferry serving Krimpen only.

From Ridderkerk ferry terminal, head diagonally across car park to leave by far corner R (De Schans). Follow road bearing L to reach 50. Turn R (Ringdijk), with flood dyke above L and follow this past shipyard and riverside houses R. By next industrial unit R, keep R alongside factory and continue on cycle track climbing onto dyke. Dog-leg L and R to join road and continue until this turns away from river behind new apartments. Bear R, fork L (Pontonweg) and immediately R (Loodspad) behind blue apartment building. After 50m bear L around crescent and where this reaches road, fork L ahead to reach main road. Follow this street (becoming Oostdijk) along top of flood dyke for 2.5km passing **Bolnes** (31km), initially on road, but moving onto cycle lane R part way. ▸

Signposts take LF11b on convoluted route through backstreets of Bolnes and under motorway bridge, rejoining part way along Bovenstraat. Route suggested here is more direct and easier to follow.

Pass shipyard and marina R, and follow road curving L, with Brienennoordbrug motorway bridge high above. Fork R (Bovenstraat) and pass under bridge. Continue over two cross routes and bear R parallel with main highway. Cross entrance to service road and continue on red asphalt cycle track along dyke between highway L and

Erasmus Bridge in Rotterdam lifting to allow a ship through

service road R. Follow track bearing R opposite **De Kuip stadium** of Feyenoord FC (33km), and continue beside highway (Laan op Zuid) for 3km, crossing railway bridge, passing mosque L and ⑥②. When Nieuwe Maas river is reached, bear L to traffic lights and turn R over spectacular **Erasmusbrug** (Erasmus Bridge), the first section of which is world's largest bascule lifting bridge. Arrive in **Rotterdam** opposite Leuvenhaven old inner harbour, now a ship museum (37km; 1m) (accommodation, refreshments, YH, tourist office, cycle shop, station).

Rotterdam (pop. 611,000), the second-largest city in the Netherlands, owes its prosperity to its position at the mouth of the Rhine–Meuse river system. The port, originally concentrated around the historic centre, now extends over 40km along the Meuse and covers 105 sq km, including reclaimed land stretching out into the North Sea. It was the world's busiest port until surpassed in 2004 by Shanghai, its main activities being the petrochemical industries

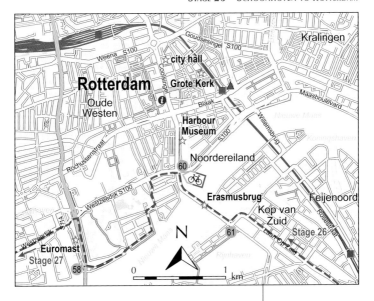

and transhipment of general container cargo from ocean-going vessels to Rhine barges.

Rotterdam has been at the forefront of European architecture since 1898, when Witte Huis, Europe's first skyscraper, was completed. Major redevelopment of the city centre since 1945 has resulted in many stunning modern buildings gracing its skyline. Rotterdam today is a cosmopolitan city with a diverse racial mix, including 80,000 Muslims and over 70,000 people from Dutch Caribbean countries.

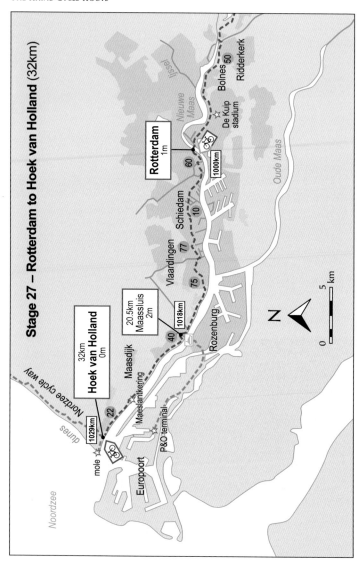

Stage 27 – Rotterdam to Hoek van Holland (32km)

STAGE 27
Rotterdam to Hoek van Holland

Start	Erasmus Bridge, Rotterdam (1m)
Finish	Ferry terminal, Hoek van Holland (0m)
Distance	32km
Signposting	LF11b Rotterdam–Vlaardingen, LF12b Vlaardingen–Hoek van Holland, with deviations

Starting from central Rotterdam, a well-defined and signposted network of cycle tracks alongside roads takes the route past the older harbour area and through Schiedam. After Vlaardingen, the riverbank is followed closely to reach Hoek van Holland ferry port. A final excursion leads across dunes to the river mouth on the North Sea shore.

At N end of Erasmus Bridge in centre of **Rotterdam** 60, turn W along cycle track on L side of Vasteland. After 300m, turn L on cycle lane along Scheepstimmermanslaan (becoming Van Vollenhovenstraat) to

Veerhaven in Rotterdam is a harbour for traditional Dutch barges

The 185m tall Euromast in Rotterdam

The 185m tall Euromast tower can be visited for the best view of Rotterdam. The top stage is in a small capsule that rises up the mast above the main viewing gallery.

This section, passing some of Rotterdam's older port facilities, is undergoing major redevelopment. The new road from Fortuynplein to Marconiplein, along the route of an old railway, is part of these works.

reach Westplein. Bear R and turn L (Veerhaven) alongside harbour filled with restored Dutch barges, to reach riverbank. Turn R (Westerkade) alongside river and continue into Parkkade to reach 58 over entrance to Maastunnel. Turn R into park and follow cycle track past base of **Euromast** tower L (2km). ◄

Reach roundabout (Droogleever Fortuynplein) and turn L crossing bridge over road from Maastunnel and lifting bridge over canal into Westzeedijk. Follow cycle track L of new road for 2.5km, bearing gently R and passing 59 Delfshaven harbour R with windmill on quayside, to reach Marconiplein. ◄

Follow cycle track round L below Europoint building, then turn R across side road and bear L on cycle track beside Schiedamseweg for nearly 2km to reach **Schiedam** 10 (7.5km) (accommodation, refreshments, tourist office, cycle shop, station).

Schiedam (pop. 75,000) is an attractive old town. Its wealth was derived from production of jenever (Dutch gin) and it is home to the Jenever Museum. Its six old windmills, formerly used for milling

A lift bridge at Schiedam, with jenever grain mill in distance

grain for gin distilling, are the world's tallest traditional mills.

Cross over road, and bear L on cycle track R of Gerrit Verboonstraat. Cross small canal bridge and continue on Oranjestraat over second, larger bridge to reach roundabout. Turn R, and after 100m turn L at next roundabout into Burgmeester Knappertlaan. Follow this for 1.3km through residential area and cross main road ahead into Vlaardingerdijk. At complicated junction shortly before metro bridge, dog-leg L over slip road and R to continue across traffic lights and under metro ⑨ and motorway bridges by Vijfsluizen station. Continue ahead under railway bridge by Vlaardingen Oost station. Turn immediately L at Burgmeester Van Lierplein ⑦⑦ into Schiedamseweg, then fork L into van Leyden Gaelstraat, quiet residential street with no cycle lane. Continue ahead along cobbled street to emerge at canal. Cross canal on lifting bridge and turn R alongside canal (Westhavenkade). Turn L on cobbled street (Dayer) into oldest part of **Vlaardingen** (12km) (accommodation, refreshments, camping, tourist office, cycle shop, station). ▶

Turn R from Dayer along Bredesteeg to reach Markt, the old square in Vlaardingen, where you will find Grote Kerk and old town hall.

Continue into Domerstraat alongside dyke R. Where this becomes Mozartlaan, climb up R onto dyke and fork R down other side to pass under road bridge. Fork L up ramp back onto dyke and turn L across main road to follow cycle track (Maassluisdijk) along top of dyke and reach (75). Cross road L at end and continue over level crossing. Bear R on cycle track alongside L of main road. Pass industrial estate L, cross Haringbuisweg then bear L over dyke and turn L on cycle track (Koggehaven) to reach riverbank. Turn R and follow riverbank for 4.5km, passing ㊷ and cafe in Oeverbos park R before dog-legging past sluices to reach Maassluis–Rozenburg ferry. Turn R on cycle track beside ferry ramp and follow road winding round to cross level crossing and reach main road at **Maassluis** (20.5km; 2m) (station). ◂

To reach P&O ferry terminal in Europoort, cross river by ferry to Rozenburg and follow LF1 to reach Europaweg. Turn R alongside main road for 9km and bear R to terminal at berth 5805 (11.5km from Maasluis).

Originally a small fishing village, **Maassluis** (pop. 32,000) became home port for Rotterdam's tugboat fleet. The last steam tugboat in the Netherlands is preserved in the town's harbour.

Turn L over canal lifting bridge, passing ㊵ and continue ahead on cycle track L of Industrieweg. Turn L (Maasweg) over level crossing and follow this between industrial units. Bear L at end, and after 100m sharply back R to regain riverbank. Continue for 6.5km, passing ㊲ then detour a few metres away from river to cross sluice gates of Oranjekanaal. After sluices, bear R below dyke L, with railway R, to pass massive gates of **Maeslantkering** storm surge barrier L (28km).

The **Maeslantkering**, one of the largest moving objects on earth, is part of the Delta Works, a vast series of dykes, sluices and flood barriers designed to protect the Netherlands from floods driven by North Sea storm surges. It consists of two steel gates that, if placed on their side, would be taller than the Eiffel Tower and weigh twice as much. These are housed in dry docks on each shore. If a storm surge over 3m above normal is forecast, the gates are swung into position and the estuary closed. It was predicted such an event could occur every 10 years. Since the barrier's completion in 1997 this has never happened, although it is closed once every autumn to test the system and on 8 November 2007 it was closed for an anticipated 2.6m surge to test the mechanism in stormy conditions.

Return to riverbank beyond flood gates and continue for 1.3km to point where cycle track turns away from river to pass behind holding park for trucks awaiting ferry to Harwich (ignore sp L 'Engeland' – it relates only to commercial vehicles). Cross level crossing and turn L 22 on top of dyke with railway L. Continue past houses below dyke R and station L. Turn sharply L over level crossing and continue straight ahead to North Sea ferry terminal at **Hoek van Holland** (32km; 0m) (accommodation, refreshments, camping, station).

North Sea extension

Having cycled this far it would be a pity not to go all the way to the sea. It is 3km from ferry terminal to end of the mole. Turn R alongside inner harbour (Stationsweg, becoming Havenweg). At T-junction turn L (Cruquiusweg) and R on cycle track beside Koningin Emma boulevard. Where cycle track turns away R, bear L across road and continue on track between river mouth and dunes. This leads to cycleable concrete **mole** extending 1km into North Sea.

Hoek van Holland, beach and dunes looking towards Den Haag

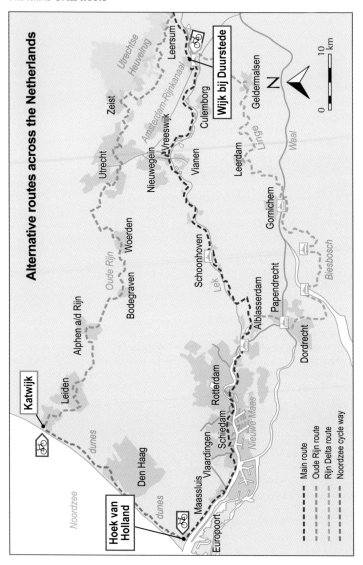

Alternative routes across the Netherlands

ALTERNATIVE ROUTES ACROSS
THE NETHERLANDS

As soon as the Rhine reaches the Netherlands it starts dividing into separate channels to reach the sea at five different points. The main route describes the direct route from Arnhem to Rotterdam. There are number of alternatives, two of which – the Oude Rijn route and the Rijn Delta route – are summarised here. Arnhem to Hoek van Holland by main route is 168km, by the Oude Rijn route 196km and by the Rijn Delta route 213km.

Oude Rijn route

Start	⑰, Amerongen (17m)
Finish	Sluice gates, Kaatwijk (0m)
Distance	114km (plus 38km to Hoek van Holland)
Signposting	LF4b (Amerongen–Bodegraven)

The Oude Rijn route follows the Oude Rijn (the oldest of all the courses and the river's exit to the sea in Roman times). This starts as Kromme Rijn near Wijk bij Duurstede, becoming Leidse Rijn in Utrecht. Our route joins it before Woerden from where, as the Oude Rijn, it is followed to the sea at Katwijk. It is LF waymarked as far as Bodegraven. From Katwijk, the Noordzee cycle way runs to Hoek van Holland.

From ⑰ in **Amerongen**, LF4 turns NW through Leersum (2km) then skirts Utrechtse Heuvelrug National Park, passing Doorn R and Odijk L, to reach **Zeist** (24km). Circling round Slot Zeist Castle, the route continues past Bunnik into the suburbs of **Utrecht**, where it passes through the old city centre (37km).

Leaving Utrecht past the railway station and over Amsterdam Rijnkanaal, LF4 continues through an area of new suburban development W of Utrecht to reach

The Oude Rijn is somewhat quieter than the Rhine

Kasteel de Haar castle. After crossing an area of open polderland, the Oude Rijn is reached at ⑦② shortly before **Woerden** (64km). The river is closely followed to **Bodegraven** (74km), where LF4 leaves the river, heading directly for Den Haag. Our route continues along the Oude Rijn towpath through **Alphen a/d Rijn** (83km) to **Leiden** (99km). Although this is not LF waymarked, it is easy to follow.

Between Leiden and Katwijk the area is mostly built-up. A well-signposted cycle route (not LF waymarked) more or less follows the river to Rijnsburg. After passing through an industrial estate, the Oude Rijn is rejoined and followed to the Noordzee (North Sea) at **Katwijk** (114km). Here the river ends at sluices designed to keep the sea out rather than allow access to the ocean. The Noordzee cycle way (LF1) runs through the coastal dunes, connecting Katwijk with Scheveningen and Den Haag (133km) and Hoek van Holland (152km).

Start	Ferry terminal, Wijk bij Duurstede (7m)
Finish	⑲, Alblasserdam (–1m)
Distance	114km (plus 16km to Rotterdam)
Signposting	LF17, LF12, LF11

The second alternative route, the Rijn Delta route, is waymarked throughout from Wijk bij Duurstede to Rotterdam. It follows the attractive Linge, another old Rhine course, before heading across the Waal and through the Biesbosch marshes to Dordrecht. It is an attractive but circuitous alternative.

From **Wijk bij Duurstede**, LF17 crosses the Lek (by ferry) and Amsterdam Rijnkanaal (by bridge) to reach **Buren** (9km) and on to **Geldermalsen** (15km). Here it picks up the narrow winding Linge river, which is followed past a series of pretty villages and **Leerdam** (36km) to reach ㉙. Turning S to the Waal at Fort Vuren (a waterline fort), the route continues into **Gorinchem** (51km).

Ferry to Woudrichem to join LF12 which winds S across flat polderland, and small ferry over the Steur, to reach **Biesbosch Nature Reserve** (82km), an area of lakes and marsh. Continuing by ferry across the Nieuwe Merwede to Kopvan 't Land, the route joins LF11 to pass through centre of **Dordrecht** (103km). After ferry to **Papendrecht**, then through stunningly pretty Oud-Alblas, the route rejoins main route at ⑲ near **Alblasserdam** (114km). From here LF11 continues to **Rotterdam** (see Stage 26; 130km).

Gentle cycling beside the Linge on the Rijn Delta route

APPENDIX A
Route summary table

Stage	Start	Finish	Distance	Signposting	Page
1	Oberalppass summit (2046m)	Ilanz square (699m)	52km	R2	43
2	Ilanz square (699m)	Chur station (585m)	35km	R2	51
3	Chur station (585m)	Buchs station (447m)	48km	R2	57
4	Buchs station (447m)	Bregenz station (398m)	56km	R2, BR	65
5	Bregenz station (398m)	Konstanz Bridge (403km)	57km (+4km)	BR, D8	73
6	Konstanz Bridge (403km)	Schaffhausen Bridge (392m)	48km	R2	83
7	Schaffhausen Bridge (392m)	Waldshut town hall (341m)	60km (49km via Lottstetten, Germany)	R2, D8	91
8	Waldshut town hall (341)	Basel Cathedral (245m)	68km	D8, R2	99
9	Basel Cathedral (263m)	Place d'Armes, Neuf-Brisach (194m)	66km	RR (with deviations)	108
10	Place d'Armes, Neuf-Brisach (194m)	Quai Louis Pasteur, Strasbourg (140m)	69km	RR (with deviations)	114
11	Quai Louis Pasteur, Strasbourg (140m)	Drusenheim ferry (124m)	33km	RR (with deviations)	120
12	Drusenheim ferry (124m)	Karlsruhe station (115m)	56km	RR (in France)	125
13	Karlsruhe station (115m)	Klipfelsau, Speyer (97m)	51km	RR (from Lemersheim)	133

Stage	Start	Finish	Distance	Signposting	Page
14	Klipfelsau, Speyer (97m)	Ludwigstrasse, Worms (91m)	49km	RR (W bank), local (E bank)	139
15	Ludwigstrasse, Worms (91m)	Mainz town hall (86m)	53km	RR	147
16	Mainz town hall (86m)	Bacharach station (79m)	48km	RR	155
17	Bacharach station (79m)	Deutsches Eck, Koblenz (65m)	50km	RR	161
18	Deutsches Eck, Koblenz (65m)	Königswinter ferry (54m)	59km	RR, D8	169
19	Königswinter ferry (54m)	Köln railway bridge (42m)	46km	RR, D8, local	177
20	Köln railway bridge (42m)	Schlossturm, Düsseldorf (35m)	52km	RR, D8, local	185
21	Schlossturm, Düsseldorf (35m)	Königstrasse, Duisburg (31m)	32km	RR, D8, local	193
22	Königstrasse, Duisburg (31m)	Xanten main square (29m)	51km	RR, D8, local	199
23	Xanten main square (29m)	Arnhem station (23m)	67km	RR, LF3b	206
24	Arnhem station (23m)	Dijkstraat, Wijk bij Duurstede (7m)	51km	LF4b	213
25	Dijkstraat, Wijk bij Duurstede (7m)	Schoonhoven ferry (−2m)	48km	local	221
26	Schoonhoven ferry (−2m)	Erasmus Bridge, Rotterdam (1m)	37km	local, LF11b	226
27	Erasmus Bridge, Rotterdam (1m)	Ferry terminal, Hoek van Holland (0m)	32km	LF11b, LF12b (with deviations)	233
Oude Rijn route	Amerongen (17m)	Kaatwijk (0m)	114km (+38km)	LF4b	239
Rijn Delta route	Wijk bij Duurstede (7m)	Alblasserdam (−1m)	114km (+16km)	LF17, LF12, LF11	241

APPENDIX B
Glossary

English	German	French	Dutch
barrier	Sperre	barrière	slagboom
bicycle	Fahrrad	vélo	fiets
bridge	Brücke	pont	brug
castle	Schloss	château	kasteel
cathedral	Dom	cathédrale	kathedraal
church	Kirche	église	kerk
cycle track	Radweg	véloroute	fietspad
cyclist	Radfahrer	cycliste	fietser
dam	Damm	barrage	dam
diversion	Umleitung	déviation	omleiding
dyke	Deich	levée	dijk
ferry	Fähre	bac	veer
field	Feld	champ	veld
floods	Hochwasser	inondation	overstromingen
forest/woods	Wald/Wälder	forêt/bois	bos
fort/fortress	Festung	fort/forteresse	vesting
lock	Schleuse	écluse	sluis
monastery	Kloster	monastère	klooster
monument	Denkmal	monument	monument
motorway	Autobahn	autoroute	autosnelweg
one-way street	Einbahnstrasse	sens unique	eenrichtingsstraat
puncture	Platte	crevaison	lekke band
railway	(Eisen)bahn	chemin de fer	spoorweg
river	Fluss	fleuve	rivier
riverbank	Ufer	rive	oever
road closed	Strasse geschlossen	route fermée	weg afgesloten
station	Bahnhof	gare	station
tourist information	Fremdenverkehrsbüro	syndicat d'initiative	VVV kantoor
town hall	Rathaus	hôtel de ville/marie	stadhuis
youth hostel	Jugendherberge	auberge de jeunesse	jeugdherberg

APPENDIX C
Useful contacts

Touring clubs
Cycle Touring Club (CTC)
0844 736 8450
cycling@ctc.org.uk
www.ctc.org.uk

ADFC (German national cycling club)
www.adfc.de

Accommodation
Youth Hostels Association
0800 0191700
customerservices@yha.org.uk
www.yha.org.uk

Hostelling International (YHA)
www.hihostels.com

Bett+Bike
www.bettundbike.de

Transport
Rail Europe (SNCF)
0844 848 4064
www.raileurope.co.uk

Deutsche Bahn (DB)
0871 8808066 (UK)
+49(0)180 5996633
www.bahn.com

Swiss Bundesbahn (SBB)
+41(0)900 300 300
www.sbb.ch

P&O Ferries
08716 642121 (UK)
+44(0)1304 863000 (outside UK)
+31(0)20 200 8333 (NL)
www.poferries.com

Stena Line
08447 70 70 70
www.stenaline.co.uk

Eurotunnel
01303 282201
www.eurotunnel.com

European Bike Express
01430 422111
info@bike-express.co.uk
www.bike-express.co.uk

Maps
Stanfords
12–14 Long Acre
London WC2E 9LP
0207 836 1321
sales@stanfords.co.uk
www.stanfords.co.uk

The Map Shop
15 High St
Upton upon Severn WR8 0HJ
0800 085 40 80 or 01684 503146
themapshop@btinternet.com
www.themapshop.co.uk

Publicpress
www.publicpress.de

Bikeline Guides
www.esterbauer.com

Veloland Swiss
www.veloland.ch

Dutch waymarking
Nederland Fietsland
www.nederlandfietsland.nl

APPENDIX D
Principal tourist offices

Ilanz
Bahnhof
+41(0)81 925 20 70
www.ilanz.ch

Chur
Bahnhof
+41(0)81 252 18 18
www.churtourismus.ch

Vaduz
Stadtle 38
+423 239 63 63
www.tourismus.li

Buchs
Bahnhof
+41(0)81 740 05 40

Bregenz
Rathausstrasse 35a
+43(0) 5574 44959 0
www.bregenz.ws

Lindau
Alfred-Nobel-Platz 1
+49(0)8382 26 00 30
www.lindau-tourismus.de

Friedrichshafen
Bahnhofplatz 2
+49(0)7541 3001 0
en.friedrichshafen.info

Konstanz
Bahnhofplatz 43
+49(0)7531 133 030
www.constance-lake-constance.com

Stein am Rhein
Oberstadt 3
+41(0)52 742 20 90
www.steinamrhein.ch

Schaffhausen
Herrenacker 15
+41(0)52 632 40 20
www.schaffhauserland.ch

Waldshut
Wallstrasse 26
+49(0)7751 833 200
www.waldshut-tiengen.de

Bad Säckingen
Waldshuter Strasse 20
+49(0)7761 5683 0
www.bad-saeckingen-tourismus.de

Rheinfelden
Marktgasse 16
+41(0)61 835 52 00
www.tourismus-rheinfelden.ch

Basel
Bahnhof
+41(0)61 268 68 68
www.basel.com

Neuf-Brisach
6 Place d'Armes
+33(0)3 89 72 56 66
www.tourisme-paysdebrisach.com

Strasbourg
17 Place de la Cathédrale
+33(0)3 88 52 28 28
www.otstrasbourg.fr

Karlsruhe
Bahnhofplatz 6
+49(0)721 3720 5383
www.karlsruhe-tourismus.de

Germersheim
Kolpingplatz 3
+49(0)7274 960260
www.germersheim.de/tourismus

Speyer
Maximilianstrasse 11
+49(0)6232 142392
www.speyer.de/de/tourist/infos

Mannheim
Willy-Brandt-Platz 3
+49(0)621 293 8700
www.tourist-mannheim.de

Ludwishafen
Berliner Platz 1
+49(0)621 512035
www.lukom.com

Worms
Neumarkt 14
+49(0)6241 25045
www.worms.de/englisch/tourismus

Oppenheim
Merianstrasse 2
+49(0)6133 49090
www.stadt-oppenheim.de

Mainz
Brueckenturm am Rathaus
+49(0)6131 286210
www.touristik-mainz.de

Rüdesheim
Geisenheimer Strasse 22
+49(0)6722 906150
www.ruedesheim.de

Bingen
Rheinkai 21
+49(0)6721 184200
www.bingen.de

Bacharach
Oberstrasse 45
+49(0)6743 919303
www.rhein-nahe-touristik.de

St Goar
Heerstrasse 86
+49(0)6741 383
www.st-goar.de

Boppard
Marktplatz (Altes Rathaus)
+49(0)6742 3888
www.boppard-tourismus.de

Koblenz
Jesuitenplatz 2
+49(0)261 130920
www.koblenz-touristik.de

Andernach
Konrad-Adenauer-Allee 40
+49(0)2632 9879480
www.andernach.de

Königswinter
Drachenfelsstrasse 51
+49(0)2223 917711
www.siebengebirge.com

Bonn
Windeckstrasse 1
+49(0)228 775000
www.bonn.de/tourismus

Köln
Kardinal-Hoffner-Platz 1
+49(0)22122 130400
www.cologne-tourism.com

Düsseldorf
Marktstrasse/Rheinstrasse
+49(0)21117 202840
www.duesseldorf-tourismus.de

Duisburg
City Palais, Königstrasse 39
+49(0)203 285440
www.duisburgnonstop.de

Xanten
Kurfürstenstrasse 9
+49(0)2801 772200
www.xanten.de/de/tourismus

Arnhem
Stationsplein 13
+31(0)481 366250
en.vvvarnhemnijmegen.nl

Wijk bij Duurstede
Markt 24
+31(0)343 575995
www.vvv-wijkbijduurstede.nl

Schoonhoven
Stadthuis straat 1
+31(0)182 385009
www.vvvschoonhoven.nl

Rotterdam
Coolsingel 195/197
+31(0) 10 271 0120
en.rotterdam.info

Youth hostels

Switzerland
Stage 1
Disentis (independent)
Cucagna, Via Alpsu 19
+41 81 929 5555

Stages 2 and 3
Chur (independent)
Welschdörfli 19
+41 81 284 1010

Stage 5 variant
Romanshorn
Gottfried-Keller-Strasse 6
+41 71 463 1717

Stage 5 variant and Stage 6
Kreuzlingen
Hornliberg, Promenadenstrasse 7
+41 71 688 2663

Stage 6
Stein am Rhein
Hemishoferstrasse 87
+41 52 741 1255

Stages 6 and 7
Schaffhausen
Belair, Randenstrasse 65
+41 52 625 8800

Stage 7
Dachsen
Schloss Laufen am Rheinfall
+41 52 659 6152

Stages 8 and 9
Basel
St Alban-Kirchrain 10
+41 61 272 0572

Liechtenstein
Stage 3
Schaan
Untere Rüttigasse 6
+423 232 5022

Austria
Stages 4 and 5
Hard
Allmendstrasse 87
+43 5574 73435

Germany
Stage 5
Lindau
Herbergsweg 11
+49 8382 96710

Stage 5
Friedrichshafen
Lindauer Strasse 3
+49 7541 72404

Stage 5
Staad (Konstanz)
Zur Allmannshöhe 16
+49 7531 32260

near to Stage 9
Breisach an Rhein
Rheinuferstrasse 12
+49 7667 7665

near to Stage 8
Kehl (Strasbourg)
Altrheinweg 11
+49 7851 2330

Stages 12 and 13
Karlsruhe
Moltkestrasse 24
+49 721 28248

Stages 13 and 14
Speyer
Geibstrasse 5
+49 6232 61597

Stage 14
Mannheim
Rheinpromenade 21
+49 621 822718

Stages 14 and 15
Worms
Dechaneigasse 1
+49 6241 25780

Stages 15 and 16
Mainz
Otto-Brunfels-Schneise 4
+49 613 85332

Stage 16
Rüdesheim
Jugendherberge 1
+49 6722 2711

Stage 16
Bingen
Herterstrasse 51
+49 6721 32163

Stages 16 and 17
Bacharach
Burg Stahleck
+49 6743 1266

Stage 17
Oberwesel
Auf dem Schönberg
+49 6744 93330

Stage 17
St Goar
Bismarckweg 17
+49 6741 388

Stages 17 and 18
Koblenz
Festung Ehrenbreitstein
+49 261 972870

Stage 18
Bad Honnef
Selhofer Strasse 106
+49 2224 71300

Stage 19
Bonn
Haager Weg 42
+49 228 289970

Stage 19
Bonn (independent)
Max, Maxstrasse 7
+49 228 82345780

Stages 19 and 20
Köln Deutz
Siegesstrasse 5
+49 221 814771

Stages 19 and 20
Köln Pathpoint
Allerheiligenstrasse 15
+49 221 13056860

Stage 20
Köln Riehl
An der Schanz 14
+49 221 767081

Stages 20 and 21
Düsseldorf (independent)
Fürstenwall 180
+49 211 3020848

Stages 20 and 21
Düsseldorf
Düsseldorfer Strasse 1
+49 211 557310

Stage 21
Duisburg Wedau
Kalkweg 148E
+49 203 724164

Stages 21 and 22
Duisburg city (independent)
Friedenstrasse 85
+49 203 9356362

Stage 22
Duisburg Meiderich
Lösorter Strasse 133
+49 203 417900

Stages 22 and 23
Xanten
Südsee, Bankscher Weg 4
+49 2801 98500

France
Stages 10 and 11
Strasbourg Deux Rives
Rue des Cavaliers
+33 3 88 45 54 20

Stages 10 and 11
Strasbourg René Cassin
Rue Auberge de Jeunesse 9
+33 3 88 30 26 46

The Netherlands
Stages 23 and 24
Arnhem
Diepenbrocklaan 27
+31 26 442 0114

Stage 24
Doorwerth
Kerklaan 50
+31 26 333 4300

Stages 26 and 27
Rotterdam
Overblaak 85–87
+31 10 436 5763

Oude Rijn route
Bunnik (Utrecht)
Rhijnauwenselaan 14
+31 30 656 1277

Rijn Delta route
Dordrecht
Baanhoekweg 25
+31 78 621 2167

Noordzee cycle way
Den Haag
Scheepmakersstraat 27
+31 70 315 7878

LISTING OF CICERONE GUIDES

Roads and Tracks of
  the Lake District
Rocky Rambler's Wild Walks
Scrambles in the Lake District
  North and South
Short Walks in Lakeland
  1 South Lakeland
  2 North Lakeland
  3 West Lakeland
The Cumbria Coastal Way
The Cumbria Way and the
  Allerdale Ramble
Tour of the Lake District

**DERBYSHIRE, PEAK DISTRICT
AND MIDLANDS**
High Peak Walks
Scrambles in the Dark Peak
The Star Family Walks
Walking in Derbyshire
White Peak Walks
  The Northern Dales
  The Southern Dales

SOUTHERN ENGLAND
A Walker's Guide to
  the Isle of Wight
Suffolk Coast and
  Heaths Walks
The Cotswold Way
The North Downs Way
The Peddars Way and
  Norfolk Coast Path
The Ridgeway National Trail
The South Downs Way
The South West Coast Path
The Thames Path
Walking in Berkshire
Walking in Kent
Walking in Sussex
Walking in the Isles of Scilly
Walking in the New Forest
Walking in the Thames Valley
Walking on Dartmoor
Walking on Guernsey
Walking on Jersey
Walking on the Isle of Wight
Walks in the South Downs
  National Park

**WALES AND WELSH
BORDERS**
Backpacker's Britain – Wales
Glyndwr's Way
Great Mountain Days
  in Snowdonia
Hillwalking in Snowdonia

Hillwalking in Wales
  Vols 1 and 2
Offa's Dyke Path
Ridges of Snowdonia
Scrambles in Snowdonia
The Ascent of Snowdon
Lleyn Peninsula Coastal Path
Pembrokeshire Coastal Path
The Shropshire Hills
The Wye Valley Walk
Walking in Pembrokeshire
Walking in the South
  Wales Valleys
Walking on Gower
Walking on the
  Brecon Beacons
Welsh Winter Climbs

**INTERNATIONAL
CHALLENGES, COLLECTIONS
AND ACTIVITIES**
Canyoning
Europe's High Points
The Via Francigena
  (Canterbury to Rome):
  Part 1

EUROPEAN CYCLING
Cycle Touring in France
Cycle Touring in Ireland
Cycle Touring in Spain
Cycle Touring in Switzerland
Cycling in the French Alps
Cycling the Canal du Midi
Cycling the River Loire
The Danube Cycleway
The Grand Traverse of
  the Massif Central
The Rhine Cycle Route
The Way of St James

AFRICA
Climbing in the Moroccan
  Anti-Atlas
Kilimanjaro
Mountaineering in the
  Moroccan High Atlas
The High Atlas
Trekking in the Atlas
  Mountains
Walking in the Drakensberg

**ALPS – CROSS-BORDER
ROUTES**
100 Hut Walks in the Alps
Across the Eastern Alps: E5
Alpine Points of VIew

Alpine Ski Mountaineering
  1 Western Alps
  2 Central and Eastern Alps
Chamonix to Zermatt
Snowshoeing
Tour of Mont Blanc
Tour of Monte Rosa
Tour of the Matterhorn
Trekking in the Alps
Walking in the Alps
Walks and Treks in the
  Maritime Alps

**PYRENEES AND FRANCE/
SPAIN CROSS-BORDER
ROUTES**
Rock Climbs in The Pyrenees
The GR10 Trail
The Mountains of Andorra
The Pyrenean Haute Route
The Pyrenees
The Way of St James
  France and Spain
Through the Spanish
  Pyrenees: GR11
Walks and Climbs in
  the Pyrenees

AUSTRIA
The Adlerweg
Trekking in Austria's
  Hohe Tauern
Trekking in the Stubai Alps
Trekking in the Zillertal Alps
Walking in Austria

EASTERN EUROPE
The High Tatras
The Mountains of Romania
Walking in Bulgaria's
  National Parks
Walking in Hungary

FRANCE
Chamonix Mountain
  Adventures
Ecrins National Park
GR20: Corsica
Mont Blanc Walks
Mountain Adventures in
  the Maurienne
The Cathar Way
The GR5 Trail
The Robert Louis
  Stevenson Trail
Tour of the Oisans: The GR54
Tour of the Queyras

For full information on all
our guides, and to order
books and eBooks,
visit our website:
www.cicerone.co.uk.

Walking – Trekking – Mountaineering – Climbing – Cycling

Over 40 years, Cicerone have built up an outstanding collection of 300 guides, inspiring all sorts of amazing adventures.

 Every guide comes from extensive exploration and research by our expert authors, all with a passion for their subjects. They are frequently praised, endorsed and used by clubs, instructors and outdoor organisations.

All our titles can now be bought as **e-books** and many as iPad and Kindle files and we will continue to make all our guides available for these and many other devices.

Our website shows any **new information** we've received since a book was published. Please do let us know if you find anything has changed, so that we can pass on the latest details. On our **website** you'll also find some great ideas and lots of information, including sample chapters, contents lists, reviews, articles and a photo gallery.

It's easy to keep in touch with what's going on at Cicerone, by getting our monthly **free e-newsletter**, which is full of offers, competitions, up-to-date information and topical articles. You can subscribe on our home page and also follow us on **Facebook** and **Twitter**, as well as our **blog**.

Cicerone – the very best guides for exploring the world.

CICERONE

2 Police Square Milnthorpe Cumbria LA7 7PY
Tel: 015395 62069 info@cicerone.co.uk
www.cicerone.co.uk